Kodjo Wuabu
Worcester 11/12
2012

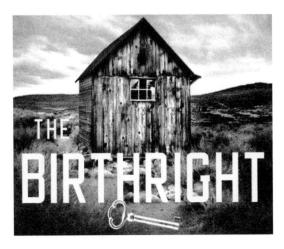

THE BIRTHRIGHT

OUT OF THE SERVANTS' QUARTERS
INTO THE FATHER'S HOUSE

JOHN SHEASBY

ZONDERVAN®

A WORTHY BOOK

ZONDERVAN.com/
AUTHORTRACKER
follow your favorite authors

ZONDERVAN

The Birthright
Copyright © 2010 by John Sheasby

Requests for information should be addressed to:

Zondervan, *Grand Rapids, Michigan 49530*

Library of Congress Cataloging-in-Publication Data

Sheasby, John.
    The birthright: out of the servant's quarters into the Father's house / John
  Sheasby.
      p. cm.
    Includes bibliographical references.
    ISBN 978-0-310-32746-2 (hardcover)
    1. Adoption (Theology) 2. Sheasby, John. 3. Christian life. I. Title.
  BT165.S54   2010
  231.7–dc22   2009051251

All Scripture quotations, unless otherwise indicated, are taken from the *New King James Version.* Copyright © 1982 by Thomas Nelson, Inc. Used by permission. All rights reserved. Verses marked AMP are taken from the *Amplified® Bible.* Copyright © 1954, 1958, 1962, 1964, 1965, 1987 by The Lockman Foundation. Used by permission. Verses marked GOD'S WORD are taken from *GOD'S WORD. GOD'S WORD* is a copyrighted work of God's Word to the Nations. Quotations are used by permission. Copyright © 1995 by God's Word to the Nations. All rights reserved. Verses marked NIV are taken from the Holy Bible, *New International Version, NIV®.* Copyright © 1973, 1978, 1984 by Biblica, Inc.™ Used by permission of Zondervan. All rights reserved worldwide. Verses marked NASB are taken from the *New American Standard Bible®.* Copyright © 1960, 1962, 1963, 1968, 1971, 1972, 1973, 1975, 1977, 1995 by The Lockman Foundation. Used by permission. Verses marked BBE are taken from *The Bible in Basic English* 1949/1964.

Packaged by Worthy Media. For subsidiary and foreign language rights contact info@worthymedia.com.

All rights reserved. No part of this publication may be reproduced, stored in a retrieval system, or transmitted in any form or by any means—electronic, mechanical, photocopy, recording, or any other—except for brief quotations in printed reviews, without the prior permission of the publisher.

Cover design: Faceout Studio, Tim Green
Cover illustration: Getty Images

Printed in the United States of America

10 11 12 13 14 15 16 /DCI/ 17 16 15 14 13 12 11 10 9 8 7 6 5 4 3 2 1

Dedicated to Beverley
The tingling touch of our hands
in Buenos Aires
Huddled together under one raincoat in the rain forest
at Victoria Falls
That electrifying kiss under the full moon
at Carmel
The geography of falling in love was prophetic
of the journey we would take together
Side by side
Like Abraham and Sarah
From Africa to America
Pilgrims, dissatisfied with normalcy
Urgently pursuing the Father's heart
You supported me
Encouraged me
Challenged me
Loved me
For forty years we have
loved
grown
even through the tough times
raised wonderful children
The best is yet to be
The joy is: you are by my side
discovering
dancing
doing the Father's will

CONTENTS

CONTENTS

FOREWORD

I first met John Sheasby about four years ago at a church in Franklin, Tennessee, where he gave a message on the material in the book you now hold in your hands. I loved his message, his passion, his South African accent. Everything about him exuded love, joy, and a peace I rarely see in most people today—even in Christians. We became fast friends, and every time he came to Nashville to speak we would hang out together, talking about our favorite subject: the Father's heart.

The message in this book is pivotal not only to my life and ministry but to the life and ministry of the church. At the heart of this message is our spiritual identity, which is the secret to our wholeness. So many people, I have found, find it difficult to believe that God loves them. They find it even more difficult to believe that God *delights* in them.

Yet he does. In spite of our sins, no matter how shameful. In spite of our struggles, no matter how often they have defeated us. In spite of our failures, personally or professionally.

You see, God doesn't relate to us as a master relates to his servants. He doesn't weigh our service to him and find it wanting, glaring down at us with a scowl on his face and withheld wages clutched in his hand. He relates to us as a father relates to his children. With understanding. And compassion. And tenderness. He loves us and delights in us, glowing at us with a smile on his face and a sparkle in his eye.

I know that love and that delight mainly because I saw it first in my own father's face. He thinks I hung the moon, my father. His face was—and still is, at seventy-seven years old—a glowing reflection of the face of my heavenly father. That's why it is easy for me to live as a son in whom God delights rather than as a servant in whom he is disappointed.

Not everyone, though, has lived with such a father, and so the reflection they received is a distorted one, if not an obscured one. That is why John's book is so important. It gives the clearest picture of our heavenly father from Jesus' own recollections, which he shares with us in the parable of the prodigal son. In that parable we see two brothers, both of whom represent where most Christians are living today—the one wallowing in the pigpen of his self-loathing, the other strutting in the well-tended fields of his self-righteousness. Both, as you will see in this book, were deceived about their identity.

The Enemy would love to deceive *you* about *your* identity. He would love to get you to believe that your identity is defined by the clubs you belong to, the neighborhood you live in, the house you own, the cars you drive, the job you have, the school your kids attend. All that is a lie. Your identity is defined not by your possessions but by your position. You are God's son, God's daughter, a member of his family. You have a place in his home and in his heart. It is an honored place. A cherished place. And it is *yours!*

I love this book. I hope you will too. More important, I hope that when you finish it you will feel the Father's love for you in a way you never have before. That love has the power not only to change the world but to change your world.

It is my prayer that it does.

Michael W. Smith

INTRODUCTION

It was a little after five, with coming-home traffic zipping down the street in front of our house, when the doorbell rang.

My wife, Bev, and I went to the door and opened it. A stranger filled the doorway with our son, Brad, a toddler, clutched in his arms. The man's eyes glared.

"Is this your son?" he snapped.

And before the *s* of our "yes" was out of our mouths, he lit into a lecture.

"He was wandering in the road—cars swerving to miss him, stopping, honking. He could have been killed!"

Bev lovingly reached for Brad, grateful he was safe. Fighting back tears, she cradled him in her arms.

Me, I showered the stranger with apologies, shook his hand, thanked him profusely, and shut the door. My heart raced; my face flushed. But the flush was followed by a deeper and redder

xiii

one as my embarrassment turned to anger and my anger to rage.

"How many times have I told you *never* to go out of the yard?" I yelled. Brad recoiled in Bev's arms, burying himself in her chest. "You deserve a good spanking, you disobedient, little..."

I was so angry that I was on the verge of reaching over and spanking him.

Instead I turned my rage toward Bev, shifting the blame to her.

"Why did you leave the gate open?"

She flinched, sheltering Brad's ears from the gale of words.

"How many times have I told you to make sure it's shut? This never would have happened if you had been more careful."

Bev shuddered and took Brad to the shelter of his bedroom.

Once the storm of emotions subsided, I plopped into a living room chair, suddenly exhausted, my head in my hands, so ashamed of myself. Where had that anger come from? I'd almost lost my son, and yet there were no arms of compassion reaching for him—not from me, anyway—no prayers of thanksgiving for his protection, no tears of joy for his return. Only rage and a torrent of words.

What had I become? What in the world had I become?

Then it dawned on me.

I had become my father.

The anger, the rage, the backhand of words slapped across the faces of anyone within reach.

He wasn't a bad man, my father. Wasn't a drunk. Wasn't a deadbeat. Wasn't considered a wife beater or a child abuser. He was, in fact, a pastor. A good husband in many ways. And in many ways a good father. But something was wrong with him. Something was wrong theologically. And something was wrong emotionally.

As with this incident on the day Brad walked out the front gate into oncoming traffic, whenever I lashed out in anger, the voice of my father came back to me. Author David Seamands once wrote: "Children are the best recorders but the worst interpreters." I'm sure that what he wrote was true of me. My sisters insist Daddy loved me deeply. In my mind, though, all I see are the whippings. All I hear are the yellings. All I feel is the shame.

Whether accurate or not, my perceptions of that reality *became* my reality.

And that reality bound me for much of my life.

One of the cords that bound me was cut with an incisive word from Dudley Hall that I first heard in a message he preached in July of 1995: "You cannot give what you have not received." The text of his message was from the passage where

Jesus instructed the Pharisees to go and learn the truth that God requires mercy, not sacrifice, from us. He went on to say the reason the Pharisees couldn't give mercy to others was that they had not received it themselves. The result was that they practiced perfectionistic rituals *for* God instead of enjoying a passionate relationship *with* God. Following this form of religion compulsively, down to tithing the mint and dill leaves from their gardens, they became intolerant of those who didn't measure up to the high standards they had set. Tithe by tithe, ritual by ritual, sacrifice by sacrifice, they molded an idol out of their acts of obedience, distorting the divine image into a God who was merciless, angry, and vindictive.

I realized that I, like the Pharisees, could not give mercy to others because I had not received it myself.

My father was a wonderful man in many respects, just as I was a wonderful man in many respects. He had served long and well in his ministry, just as I had served long and well in mine. He grew up in a poor farm family with eleven dirt-faced children, wearing a tatter of hand-me-down clothes and some terrible hand-me-down habits—one of which was the way children were disciplined. His father was angry and explosive, once beating him with an iron rod for disobeying. He was a hard man, my grandfather, his back bent by the plow, his face weathered by the sun, his forehead furrowed from the worries of feeding so many hungry kids, providing clothes for their backs, putting a roof over their heads.

He wasn't a bad man, my father's father, wasn't a drunk or a deadbeat, wasn't considered a wife beater or a child abuser. He was, in fact, a good, God-fearing Christian.

It was a hardscrabble life my father had. Hardscrabble lessons were preached at you, yelled at you, and, if need be, beaten into you. In order to be right with my grandfather, you had to keep up with your chores. Fail to feed the chickens, and before long, they'd fail to feed you. Forget to milk the cows one day, and forget about butter on your bread the next.

In the same way, in order to be right with God, you had to keep up with the chores he laid out for you: attend church regularly, read your Bible daily, give faithfully, and so forth—a to-do list spanning both Testaments.

If you dropped a stitch somewhere, slacked off a little here, slowed down a little there, who knew but that you might end up left behind when Jesus returned to take the faithful home with him.

That theology was passed down from my grandfather to my father to me.

The result of this strict theology—and how sternly it was applied—was fear. I was terrified of displeasing a God who was prone to outbursts of anger. Every day I was afraid. I was afraid of God smacking me for stepping out of line, singling me out and shaming me in front of the church, shunning me in some way. Condemnation and guilt followed me through life like strays, nipping at my heels and threatening to trip me up.

I look back over my journals, and they are filled with the frustration of not being able to please God. Year after year that frustration mounted, until it became insurmountable. My relationship with God became a chronicle of one failure after another. I had no joy in serving him. And I had no strength to continue a joyless, loveless relationship with a God who seemed impossible to reach and even more impossible to please.

In 1981, I resigned, leaving my pastoral ministry in Gweru, Zimbabwe.

On January 2, 1982, I pulled a travel trailer to a seaside resort near the mouth of the Igoda River in East London, South Africa. For a month I sequestered myself there, determined—like Jacob wrestling with the angel at the River Jabbok—not to give up until God blessed me with a new understanding of my relationship with him.

In that trailer by the river, he met me.

The struggle was intense.

When dawn finally came, my life was transformed.

The book you are about to read is how that transformation happened to me . . . and how it can happen to you.

An Opening Prayer from the Author

Dear heavenly Father,

Thank you for the transforming truth you used to liberate me
      in that trailer by the river
            so many years ago.
Thank you for allowing me to see the damage I was inflicting
      on my family . . .
        and for not allowing that damage to continue.
Generation after generation it continued,
      father after father,
           with such tragic results.
Yet it stopped with me.
By your mercy, it stopped with me.
As a result, my children can live free, love free, serve free,
      without condemnation or guilt.
And their children after them . . . and their children . . .
   for who knows how many generations.
Words are not adequate to praise you
      for turning my frustration into relaxation,
        my anxiety into peace,
           my drudgery into joy.
Thank you for taking me out of a perfectionistic,
    performance-based religion

to enjoy a passionate, mercy-based relationship
with you.
Now, as the readers of this book continue through these pages,
grant that your Holy Spirit would
come alongside them,
teaching them, encouraging them, consoling them.
Fill them not with regret for their past but with
hope for their future,
with the assurance that though they can't go back
to change the beginning of their story,
they can begin now to change
the ending.

In Jesus' merciful name I pray,
amen

PART I

THE SERVANT

The Motivation of the Servant

Jesus answered them, "Most assuredly, I say to you . . . a slave does not abide in the house forever, but a son abides forever. Therefore if the Son makes you free, you shall be free indeed."

John 8:34-36

Daddy was a preacher. A blowtorch of a preacher. He made Jonathan Edwards' sermon on the fires of hell—"Sinners in the Hands of an Angry God"—sound like a feel-good, flannel-board talk for preschoolers.

Two of his sermons, in particular, singed my childhood conscience.

One of them was on the Second Coming. He taught that between the travail leading up to the Second Coming and the tribulation following it came the Rapture—a doctrine that said the faithful would be caught up in the air to meet Christ, missing the wrath of God that would be poured out on all the earth. Seething cauldrons of wrath. Bowl after bowl of it. Spilling onto everyone and everything. Burning away flesh from bones. Reducing entire cities to cinders.

Not exactly the type of message that endears an eleven-year-old to religion.

The Rapture was the way out of all that. And so, as a kid not wanting to end up like the unsuspecting residents of Pompeii when Vesuvius erupted—belching plumes of smoke into the air, burying the city in ash, and sealing it over with a burning lake of lava—I prayed my knees off. Cringing before the Almighty. Confessing every sin, however small. Vowing to do better the next day. Doing everything I could to prove myself faithful.

After all, who wants to be left behind?

Those were the thoughts I carried with me day after day, a backpack of guilt and condemnation slumping the narrow shoulders of my spirit. On one such day, I took the short, four-hundred-yard walk from Orange Grove Primary School to my home on Settlers Way in Greenfields, a suburb of East London, South Africa. I loved coming home. Loved swinging open the front door. Loved the smells coming from the kitchen, a simmering pot of something on the stove. Loved the sight of my parents, the sound of their voices as they greeted me. It was such a secure feeling.

On this particular day, though, when I called to my parents, announcing that I was home, no one answered. The house was empty and still. I darted from room to room. My dad wasn't there. My mom wasn't there. My sisters weren't there.

Suddenly it hit me. Jesus had returned. Had caught up all the faithful to meet him in the air. And I . . .

I had been *left behind*.

Flashbacks of unfaithfulness flickered before my eyes—sins of commission and omission, things I had done, things I had left *un*done. The sassy words I had said. The loose change I hadn't put in the offering plate, spending it instead on penny candy. The unread Bible. The unsaid prayers. Nickel and dime stuff, mostly. But, as I suddenly realized, it added up.

As it turned out, this kid was cut a break. Jesus hadn't returned. I wasn't left behind to burn on the barbeque of the Antichrist. Eventually I found my family, ate my dinner, and, as I lay me down to sleep . . . prayed the Lord my soul to keep . . . I peacefully rested the night away.

Only to wake up the next morning to face the fear of another day.

The other sermon that struck fear into me was one that Daddy preached periodically to those slouching from grace

5

in the back pews. Their nodding attention was wakened with a raised voice and the stern words from Hebrews: "Holiness, without which no one will see the Lord" (12:14). He would pause, peer across the pews to the back row, then punctuate the verse with a sweeping gesture, a glare so intense it could peel paint off a wall, and the words: *"No one!"*

"No one" would echo within me, reverberating through the rest of the week. *No one. And that means you, little boy! You, there, the preacher's kid. Who do you think you're fooling? You're not holy. Not even close. So what makes you think* you'll *see the Lord?*

Being eleven years old, on the cusp of puberty, is reason enough for a kid to feel insecure. Add in the threat of losing your salvation, and it's not only a recipe for a fearful childhood but a failed adulthood.

So what was a kid to do?

I walked the aisle, of course, altar call after altar call, to wash away my sins. Like the instructions "Wash, rinse, repeat" on a bottle of shampoo, the instructions for my spiritual cleansing were "Repent, recommit, repeat." I wanted to be holy, to be ready, to be sure. But I never really knew I was saved, was never sure of it, never secure in it.

If the Sunday sermons didn't do me in, the weekday incriminations did. "You're not acting like a Christian," Daddy would tell me when I stepped out of line. *Whenever* I stepped out of line. I put a freshly sharpened number 2 pencil to my life and did the math. If my *assurance* of salvation was based on my *acting* like a Christian—which I interpreted as living an exemplary life of holiness—I had no hope, either of being saved or of seeing the Lord.

An eleven-year-old without hope is a sadness waiting to mature into a full-grown tragedy. Where there should have been joy, there was fear. Where there should have been affirmation, there was condemnation. Where there should have been a free spirit, full of play and flights of imagination, there was an enslaved spirit, full of guilt and feelings of insecurity.

How about *your* childhood?

"Sticks and stones may break my bones, but words will never hurt me" is a lie we were all told in our youth. The truth is we get over the sticks and stones and hurt bones; we don't get over the words. We don't get over the barrage of criticisms and sarcasms. We don't get over the verbal jabs, the put-downs, the smack-downs. And we don't get over the Sunday sermons or the weekday incriminations.

The hurt that those words inflict stays with us. My hurt did. I suspect yours did too. The fears, the insecurities, the guilt, the shame, the hopelessness—they're all still with us. They followed us from our childhoods into our adulthoods. Into our families. Into our Christian lives. Into our ministries.

The result?

A life full of insecurity, fear, and condemnation.

And I was only eleven.

Along the way to growing up, I passed through a fearful adolescence into a fearful adulthood, entered a fearful academic institution and ended up in a fearful ministerial vocation. No matter how old I got, where I went, what I did, fear was my constant traveling companion. I never felt good enough, obedient enough, holy enough. Never felt I did enough. And never felt that what I had done was good enough.

In 1978, after reflecting on a seminar I'd attended in Johannesburg taught by Arthur Glasser of Fuller Theological Seminary, I felt enough was enough. That is when I first considered resigning from pastoral ministry. We got an invitation to pastor a church in Zimbabwe, though, and I thought perhaps the change might be good for me, for Bev, for our kids.

I was wrong. After three years there, I still had the same fears, the same insecurities, the same feelings of shame. Frustrated, I admitted my defeat and decided to resign.

As if I needed further evidence of my failure, the treasurer of our church came by one day and told me he wasn't getting anything from my ministry. Later that day, my fiercest critic hand delivered a scathing letter, telling me off and informing me that my ministry was over. The next day, an elder and his wife came to me, distraught, telling me that they were no longer being fed through my ministry.

After that, I couldn't have stayed if I'd wanted to.

In September of 1981, I resigned. Bev knew I was unhappy and had been for years; she knew it was the right decision. But she was afraid. Afraid for our future, mostly, fearing how we would provide for our two children—Tracy, who was six, and Brad, who was now four.

When I told the church, I'm certain a few were relieved. Far more were resentful. Resigning at a time when many were leaving Zimbabwe because of the political upheaval, I was looked at as a captain who was deserting a sinking ship, leaving the men, women, and children on board to fend for themselves in the shark-infested waters.

In December of 1981, Bev, the kids, and I moved back to South Africa and went to live with her parents. January 2, 1982, I drove our car, pulling a small travel trailer, to the mouth of the Igoda River, where I parked under a spreading mimosa tree. From the trailer I could see the river meandering to the ocean. And from there I began a month-long struggle to find out who I was, who God was, and what the Christian life was really about.

At the time I was reading the story of Jacob, with whom I identified, hoping against hope that Igoda would be my

Bethel, the place of my encounter with God and the place of my transformation. God knows I needed it. On the sixth of January, I read Isaiah 65:13–14: "My servants will eat…my servants will drink…my servants will rejoice…My servants will sing out of the joy of their hearts" (NIV).

After reading those words, I wrote in my journal, *Lord, at this moment I have no real joy in Jesus. The song is missing in my life! O Lord, restore to me the joy of my salvation.*

Along with my journal, I had brought my Bible, some reference books, and a commentary by Dr. D. Martyn Lloyd-Jones titled *Romans: The Sons of God*. I read, I studied, I prayed, I fasted. I would wake up at seven a.m., have some tea, read my devotions, then take a break and jog for three miles along the beach. I would come back drenched in sweat, eager to grab hold of the biblical text and wrestle with it the way Jacob wrestled with the angel.

The first week was an exhausting ordeal. A lot of confusion and crying during the day. A lot of tossing and turning at night. There were moments I felt I was getting somewhere, only to be thrown on the ground, my face in the dirt, pinned by some muscular moment from my past, its mouth pressed to my ear, taunting me with guilt and shame.

And then, after dislocating a hip in my theology, God brought a dawn of understanding. It came while I was studying

John, chapter 8: "A slave does not abide in the house forever, but a son abides forever" (v. 35).

In that passage Jesus was speaking to new believers, showing them the difference between their relationship to God under the old covenant and under the new. Under the old covenant they were subject to the Law of Moses, which was designed to reveal their inability to be approved by God through their works. Because of the new covenant, they had a new position, Jesus said, and, by implication, a new motivation. The old position—that of a servant—was an inferior relationship. The new position—that of a son—was superior in every way, including motivation.

The motivation of a son serving his father was love, while the motivation of a slave serving his master was fear. The consequences of failing to do his master's will motivated the servant to fulfill that will meticulously. As a result, he lived in a constant state of insecurity, fearing the hour of reckoning, dreading his master would find fault with him and punish him.

Regardless, though, of whether the servant succeeded at his tasks or failed at them, at the end of the day he had to leave the master's house and retreat to the servants' quarters. No matter how well he performed his duties, at the end of the day it was his status, not his service, that distinguished him, determining not only where he stayed but how long he stayed there.

11

In contrast to the tenuous nature of the servant-master relationship, Jesus declared that a son "abides forever." He had a room in his father's house, a place at his table, a share in his business. His position was permanent. His place was secure. And he never had to fear losing any of those things, because all of those things were his by virtue of his birth. His status distinguished him, determining not only how near he was to the father but how dear he was to the father's heart.

—

Jesus came to liberate us, not only from our enslavement to sin but also from our employment as servants, loosing us from servitude under a covenant of law and leading us to freedom under a covenant of grace: "Therefore if the Son makes you free, you shall be free indeed" (John 8:36).

If Jesus came to free us from fear-motivated servitude and bring us into the enjoyment of our position as sons, why do so many believers still see themselves as servants, living in fear of displeasing God and incurring his wrath?

The answer to that question came to me at Igoda, from a passage in Romans 8:15: "For you did not receive the spirit of bondage again to fear, but you received the Spirit of adoption by whom we cry out, 'Abba, Father.'"

The verse puzzled me. *Why did Paul use the word "again"?* I wondered. I thought a long time about it, and then the Holy Spirit opened my eyes to all that one little word meant. Think with me through Paul's logic.

When Paul became a Christian, the law of the Spirit did not condemn him for his failure to measure up. "There is therefore now no condemnation," he declared (8:1). Instead of pointing out Paul's sin, the Spirit pointed him to his "life in Christ Jesus" (8:2). The Holy Spirit imparts life to us in place of the death that comes through the Mosaic Law. He will never minister law and condemnation to us because that always produces death: "The letter kills, but the Spirit gives life" (2 Cor. 3:6).

Instead, the Spirit's ministry to the believer is to show us the fullness of life that is ours in Christ Jesus. This revelation acts as a mirror in which we see the ways that we fall short of the life in Jesus. Then, as we come into agreement with that, he guides us out of the bondage of sin and into the freedom of life in Christ Jesus.

However, anyone who has been a Christian for any time at all will have discovered that there are people who desire to put you back under law. Some do this intentionally, as did the false teachers that Paul talked about in Galatians 3:1. Others do this unintentionally. It is possible that the person who prayed with you when you received Jesus as Savior encouraged you with words such as these: "Now that you are a Christian, you

13

need to read the Bible, pray, attend church, witness, and give." That is not bad advice because those are ways in which your new life should be expressed. The problem is that "you need" is often taken as "you must." When that happens, we are brought into bondage . . . "again." We receive a "spirit of bondage" the moment we go back to trying to gain God's approval on the basis of what we do rather than on the basis of who we are. That well-intentioned advice, given to us when we first became believers and later turned into a commandment, leads to motivation by fear.

Paul said, "You did not receive the spirit of bondage again to fear." We can correctly translate the last phrase as "leading to fear." What fear was Paul talking about? The fear of punishment that comes with not keeping the law.

"There is no fear in love; but perfect love casts out fear, because fear involves torment. But he who fears has not been made perfect in love" (1 John 4:18). John makes a bold statement: "There is no fear in love." Why is that? "Because," he said, "fear involves torment"—or, more accurately, fear involves punishment. The only one who fears is the one who doesn't understand the finished work of Jesus in paying the penalty of our sin. That means that since he took the punishment for our sin, we need not fear being punished.

"Perfect love casts out fear." The presence of fear indicates the absence of love. Therefore, if I have fear, that is the surest sign that I do not understand my position as a son and am still in bondage to performance by trying to please God and be accepted through my obedience to commandments. Fear enters when I feel that I am not reaching the acceptable standard of performance and consequently might be punished.

As an heir of the new covenant, you are no longer a servant. You are a son or a daughter, the apple of your Father's eye. As his child, you have nothing to fear. The punishment for your shortcomings and your sins, for your frailties and your failures, for the bad things you have done and for the good things you have left *un*done—all those debts were paid for at the cross.

Though our heavenly Father will not punish us, he *will* discipline us. His discipline is proof of his love for us and not to be feared by us, for it is redemptive, not punitive. It does not look back in anger at what we have done but looks forward in anticipation of who we will become.

Which is like Jesus.

As the writer to the Hebrews said:

And you have forgotten the exhortation which speaks to you as to sons:

> *"My son, do not despise the chastening of the LORD,*
> *Nor be discouraged when you are rebuked by Him;*

For whom the LORD loves He chastens,
And scourges every son whom He receives."

If you endure chastening, God deals with you as with sons; for what son is there whom a father does not chasten? But if you are without chastening, of which all have become partakers, then you are illegitimate and not sons. Furthermore, we have had human fathers who corrected us, and we paid them respect. Shall we not much more readily be in subjection to the Father of spirits and live? For they indeed for a few days chastened us as seemed best to them, but He for our profit, that we may be partakers of His holiness. (12:5–10)

Allow me to get personal for a moment.

What motivates *you?* Fear or love? Do you identify with how I lived for thirty-five years, fearing God's displeasure, feeling the frustration of never being sure that you have done enough to please him? Are your prayers filled with repeated confessions of your failures? Do you find yourself constantly promising to do better? Do you find yourself wondering if you have committed the "unpardonable sin" and dreading facing God some day?

If your answer to these questions is yes, you have probably received the spirit of bondage again, and again fear has filled your heart. Fear and love are mutually exclusive. Just as love

16

drives out fear, fear drives out love. In doing so, it also drives out the security, the peace, and the joy that the Father's love provides.

Jesus came not simply to deliver us *from* something; he came to deliver us *to* something. And that something is the Father's heart. He came not simply to deliver us *from* servitude; he came to deliver us *to* sonship. He came not simply to free us *from* fear; he came to free us *to* love.

And when the Son has set you free, you are free indeed—free to live with love and to grow up without condemnation.

Free to run.

Free to stumble.

Free to fall.

For as the heavens are high above the earth,

So great is His mercy toward those who fear Him;

As far as the east is from the west,

So far has He removed our transgressions from us.

As a father pities his children,

So the LORD pities those who fear Him.

For He knows our frame;

He remembers that we are dust. (Ps. 103:11–14)

Heal me from my childhood hurts,

    from words that ever hurt me,

        with all their subtle insinuations and unspoken implications.

Deliver me from damaged emotions and distorted perceptions.

Help me to move out of the servants' quarters

    into your house;

        out of the drudgery of doing

            into the joy of being.

Help me to realize that I am an heir, not a hired hand;

        a son, not a servant.

Help me to realize that sonship is established by paternity,

    not performance.

Whenever an accusatory voice puts me down,

    may your Spirit lift me up,

        reminding me from your Word

            that there is no condemnation for those who are

            in Christ Jesus.

And if there is no condemnation, there is no guilt.

If there is no guilt, there is no shame.

If there is no shame, there is no fear.

If there is no fear, there is no insecurity.

Because of that, I can live securely, confidently, hopefully, with youthful enthusiasm and playful abandon,

in the skipping awareness that I am loved

simply because I am yours.

All yours. And *only* yours.

Help me to see the sparkle in your eyes when you watch me wake,

the smile on your face when you follow me through the day,

the delight in your voice when you lay me down to sleep.

And may seeing those things in you

cause me to look at myself with the same sparkle in my eyes,

the same smile on my face,

the same delight in my voice.

If only I could see myself that way, Lord,

perhaps then the wolf in me can lie down with the lamb,

perhaps then, at last, I can be at peace with who I am.

And perhaps then, I can be free to love and to live,

free to run,

free to stumble,

free to fall,

knowing that however far I fall,

underneath me are your loving arms,

waiting to pick me up,

dust me off,

draw me close.

The Mind-Set of the Servant—Task Oriented

CHAPTER TWO

But he answered his father, "All these years I've worked like a slave for you. I've never disobeyed one of your commands. Yet, you've never given me so much as a little goat for a celebration with my friends."

Luke 15:29 (GOD'S WORD)

Damaged emotions lead to distorted perceptions.

My distortion?

I saw myself as a servant, not a son.

The difference between the two?

A servant's relationship to his master was task oriented. His daily responsibility consisted of entering his master's house, receiving his assignments, and performing them to the best of his ability. Should he fulfill his duties, he was rewarded. He could then retire to the servants' quarters, satisfied with his wage, confident that the relationship was secure. Should he fall short of his duties, he would be berated and sometimes beaten. His wages could be withheld, his privileges withdrawn. His employment could be terminated; in extreme cases, *he* could be terminated. The relationship with his master was tenuous because it was conditional.

In contrast to the servant, the son served as a *consequence* of the relationship, not as a *condition* of the relationship. He loved and respected his father, serving not to perform for him but to please him. Serving faithfully. Diligently. Often going above and beyond the work the servant did.

At times, though, the son failed to fulfill his responsibilities, sometimes neglecting them, even shirking them. The father might be disappointed with his son's behavior, admonish him for it, even discipline him for it. But that didn't change the relationship. The father remained the father, regardless of the son's failure, and the son remained the son, regardless of his father's disappointment. Why? Because the relationship was not based on performance; it was based on paternity.

When a child is born, it can never be *un*born. That is true in the physical realm. It is also true in the spiritual realm. Once a son, always a son.

Living as a servant under the oppressive taskmaster of the law was not only a fearful way to live, it was a frustrating way to live. Jesus, on a mission to free us from that enslavement, showed how futile such a life was: "So likewise you, when you have done all those things which you are commanded, say, 'We are unprofitable servants. We have done what was our duty to do'" (Luke 17:10).

If you see yourself as a servant and believe that your acceptance by God is based on your performance, you will be frustrated. Though you do all you believe God has commanded you to do, you will never escape the nagging feeling that you should have done more.

Fear-driven performance not only leads to frustration, it also leads to introspection. My journal entries during my seven years (1974–1981) of pastoral ministry in Pretoria, South Africa, and in Gweru, Zimbabwe, reveal an obsessive-compulsive pattern of self-evaluation and self-condemnation. Two months before going to Igoda River, I wrote:

November 1, 1981

Where I am at spiritually:
(1) Barren and dry within with no real intimate fellowship with God.
(2) My prayer life is nothing.
(3) I am bound and inhibited, without real spiritual freedom and spontaneity.

(4) I am very precise and correct in exegeting and understanding the Word but lack the Holy Spirit's interpretation to my heart.

(5) I do not know a sensitivity to the Holy Spirit. I seldom hear His voice.

(6) I am a hypocrite!

(7) I am so unchristlike in many areas: anger, impatience, irritation, and unkindness (all selfish motives). I AM CARNAL, NOT SPIRITUAL!

My last day of critical self-evaluation took place in the travel trailer at Igoda River. I was reading the story of Jacob, and in response to the angel's question to Jacob—*What is your name?* (see Gen. 32:27)—I wrote:

January 7, 1982

a. Proud b. Lustful c. Deceitful d. Angry e. Unloving f. Prayerless g. Spiritually insensitive h. Disobedient

Accusatory adjectives, each and every one of them, all pointing to a distorted sense of identity. I identified myself by my attitudes and my actions, all of them negative. Why? Because I saw myself as a servant. And as a servant, I felt I never measured up.

How do *you* see yourself?

Take a minute for self-evaluation, describing where you are spiritually:

Date: _____

1. _____
2. _____
3. _____
4. _____
5. _____
6. _____
7. _____

Now ask yourself: *What is my name?* And write a list of adjectives that describe the person you perceive yourself to be.

a. _____
b. _____
c. _____
d. _____
e. _____
f. _____
g. _____
h. _____

Take a step back from those two mirrors. What do you see?

Do you see a servant . . . or a son or daughter? Is it an accurate image of who you are . . . or a distorted one?

—

If your perceptions of yourself are distorted, how did they get that way? What happened? And when? What emotions were damaged? And how? What words came down on you like a ruler rapping the hand of a child? And who spoke them?

My father loved me. But my father's words were swift and hard and came down on me with a sharp and sudden sting. My mother loved me too. But her words also stung, leaving welts and at times breaking the skin of the sensitive boy I once was.

"Have you done your homework? Have you done your piano practice? You cannot go out and play until you have completed both."

Those were the late-afternoon words of my father, strictly and sternly spoken. As a busy pastor, he would often not be home when I returned from school. When he did come home, I dreaded the first words out of his mouth, which always felt like an inquisition. His expectations chafed me like a starched Sunday collar. I had had enough school for the day, enough rules, enough routines. I wanted to go outside with the other kids, free to run, free to play.

But no, not this kid. This kid had pages to read, scales to practice, lessons to perform. After all, this kid was a preacher's kid, and no one—least of all the preacher—was cutting him any slack.

The effect of these daily encounters was that I began to see my relationship to my father as one that was centered on tasks. If I succeeded at the tasks, I gained his approval. If I failed, I got his wrath, which was sometimes a swat with a Bible verse, other times a spanking with a bamboo cane.

Come report-card time, there was seldom a word of praise. The A's got overlooked. It was the B's that got noticed. And anything less than an "Excellent" in my behavior got me in trouble big time. My father's generation believed that giving a child praise would feed "the ugly serpent of pride." And so I seldom got any. For anything.

Another effect of those encounters was that I learned how to lie. I learned how to ever so slightly shade the truth, telling him I had finished my homework when I meant I was done with it for the day and would pick up where I left off in the morning. Of course, if he ever found out, there was the devil to pay.

I lied to avoid being found out so I wouldn't get punished, but after a while I gave up lying. I gave up a lot of things. Gave up trying to live up to my father's expectations. Gave up trying to please him, trying to make him proud.

Being the son of the pastor, exemplary behavior was expected of me. I learned to play that game too. I learned how to conform to everyone's expectations, at least outwardly. Inwardly, though, I knew it was a sham, knew I was a hypocrite. Knowing who I really was filled me with shame, and I became reclusive, fearing the rejection that exposure of my duplicity would bring.

I spent a lot of energy on the appearances of holiness, all the while fearing that someday someone would chip away at the surface and cause the entire facade to crumble. Because of that, I never allowed anyone to get close to me for fear they would see what a fake I was.

My father gave what he had received. To be fair, that's all he could have given. He was one of eleven children, raised in poverty, and every child had responsibilities around the fruit orchards and at the alluvial diamond diggings on the banks of the Vaal River. Their day started early with chores until it was time for their father to row them across the river to attend school. When they came home, there were more chores. His relationship to his father was task oriented. They were hard tasks, and his father was a hard taskmaster. It is no surprise that my father related to me in the same way his father had related to him.

It was inevitable that I saw my relationship to God in the same light. There could be only one reason for him to have saved me—slacker that I was, liar that I was, hypocrite that I was—and that was to send me out into the field of ministry to serve him. If I was ever to gain his approval, I would have to be up at dawn, quick in my boots, and hard at my chores.

My frustrations piled up during the years of my youth ministry, the years of my theological education, and the years of my pastoral ministry. My journals reflected the growing dissatisfaction I felt with the unfulfilling life I was experiencing in serving God. But the entry for June 4, 1981, marked a turning point.

It was a cool winter's day, bright with sun. I spent the day fasting, hoping to meet with God on a large cattle ranch that belonged to a dear friend who was a deacon in the church I pastored. My times of prayer and study on his ranch were some of the best I had ever had with the Lord. I had planned this day because I was desperate to break out of the performance-based prison I was in. I was starved to experience the intimacy that others seemed to enjoy, an intimacy that eluded me.

My entry for that day began with yet another exercise in self-absorption. Then I turned to Luke 10. As I read the story of Jesus' visit to Martha's home, I knew that God was speaking to me—it was the part of the story where Martha was described as distracted by all the preparations that had to be made.

In studying Martha's distraction, I found my own. I, too, was drawn off from what was central because, like her, I was convinced that doing things for Jesus was more important than being with him. That mind-set made me, as it had made Martha, anxious and troubled about so many things. After years of such thinking, I felt victimized by the ministry. I began to resent the people I served. I hated the telephone because its shrill ring represented another situation of human need that I was expected to meet. But who would meet *my* need? I was angry at the entire religious system that had trapped me into such an unfulfilling life of service.

Like Martha, I lived with an inner anxiety and agitation. But unlike Martha, I never exploded publicly. I had too much pride in my outward image for that. I did explode privately, though. My wife suffered from my angry outbursts. So did my children.

The story of Martha parallels the story of the older brother in the parable of the prodigal son. The younger son in the parable squandered his life in the distant country while the older son squandered his life at home, serving his father not as a son but as a servant, and a proud one at that: "All these years I've worked like a slave for you. I've never disobeyed one of your commands" (Luke 15:29 GOD'S WORD).

The parable reflected the Pharisees' concept of their relationship to God. Institutional Christianity's relationship to God is similar to that of the older brother. It is task oriented, based on obligations to attend, to give, and to be involved in the programs of the institution. This subverts Jesus' teaching on the individual and the institution. If the words are true that Jesus spoke in Mark 2:27—"The Sabbath was made for man, and not man for the Sabbath"—then it follows that the church was made for mankind, not mankind for the church. Religion exalts the institution and makes the individual subservient to it. Ministry is a wonderful avenue for individuals to express their love for God and for others, but when it becomes task oriented, it becomes a burdensome obligation.

Which is what ministry had become to me.

I needed a different way of doing ministry, a different motivation for serving in ministry, and a different mind-set for looking at ministry. God wanted to teach me those things, but to do so, he needed to slow me down long enough for me to hear him.

In November 1988, I was in a motel room in Memphis, where I was preaching, and I felt the Holy Spirit speaking, trying to get my attention, directing me to take a year off from ministry. With Bev's blessing, I did. During that year, I asked a lot of questions, both of the way I had been doing ministry and of the way Jesus had done it.

Wasn't my purpose in life to serve the Lord? I asked myself. *Since I was called to preach and teach, would not doing anything else be a waste of my life?* I reasoned. *If Jesus' purpose in coming to earth was to minister as the Messiah and ultimately lay down his life so that mankind might be saved, why did he waste so much time in what religion would see as the frivolous, worldly pursuit of working in the carpenter shop in his hometown of Nazareth? How many souls died without hearing his life-saving words during those wasted years where he didn't preach one sermon, didn't perform one miracle, didn't make one disciple, didn't save a single soul?*

All the questions puzzled me, and I wondered, *Could there be any higher motivation in Jesus' life than to seek and to save the lost?*

The answer came clearly in my study of John 5, beginning with verse 19. When Jesus was criticized for healing on the Sabbath, he told his critics that he did only what he saw the Father doing. As a son, his greatest delight was to do his Father's will. He equated it to eating a satisfying meal. During what seemed like wasted years of inactivity, Jesus was totally in the Father's will. For him to have attempted ministry before the Father's time would have been the real waste.

Martha's frantic activity to prepare the meal for Jesus was a waste. Jesus said that only one thing was needed and Mary had chosen what was essential. The older brother's life of diligent work and scrupulous obedience was a waste. There were well cared for servants who could have done the work while the son enjoyed being with his father, only doing what his father asked him to do instead of spending his life doing what he *thought* his father wanted.

How much time and money are wasted in so many churches doing so many good things with so few ever stopping to discover what the Father really wants from them?

As my sabbatical year in 1989 continued, I felt a release coming to my spirit, freeing me from the compulsion of performance and from the obligation of ministry at every opportunity. Finally, on August 7, as I was mowing the lawn, I stopped and said to the Lord, "Father, if you never let me preach again, that's okay with me."

Immediately I felt him say to me, "Son, if you never preach again, that's okay with me."

Then it hit me. I never again *had* to preach! Preaching was no longer my identity. I was a son, and as a son I could preach because I knew that was what the Father called me to do. But no longer was my preaching motivated by the fear of displeasing God if I didn't preach or by the guilt of what might happen to those to whom I didn't preach.

I felt the way the woman must have felt who had been bent over by a crippling disability when Jesus healed her, lifting the burden that had been on her back for eighteen years (see Luke 13:13). Suddenly I could stand up straight. As I did, everything looked different. God looked different. People looked different. I looked different. When I looked at myself in the mirror, I was surprised at the image staring back at me. It was no longer a distorted image. It was a true reflection of who I was—a dearly beloved son.

And, as I looked at that son, I saw on his face—for the first time in a long time—a smile.

Change my mind-set, Lord.

Take me out of the kitchen, where I have served in
   distraction from you,
   and bring me to your feet, where I can sit in adoration of you.
Take me out of your field, where I have worked for you,
   and bring me into your house, where I can feast with you.
Help me to not believe the distorted perceptions
      I sometimes have of myself.
Help me to understand where those distortions came from.
Give me the strength to go back to my past,
   back to the damaged emotions that led to those distortions.
Go with me, Lord, won't you?
It's so hard for me to go alone.
Go with me there and help me there.
Help me to understand what was said, who said it, and why.
Help me to understand that none of us can give what we haven't
   first received.
And in that understanding,
   help me to forgive them the way you have forgiven me,
      giving them the same grace you first gave to me.

The Mind-Set of the Servant—Reward Focused

CHAPTER THREE

But he answered his father, "All these years I've worked like a slave for you. I've never disobeyed one of your commands. Yet, you've never given me so much as a little goat for a celebration with my friends."

Luke 15:29 (GOD'S WORD)

Before my transformation in that trailer by the river, I longed to know the life of victory and joy that I had read about in books and heard about from visiting ministers who stayed at our house. I believed that if I just served diligently, prayed intensely, harbored no unconfessed sin, and if I had been thorough in making right any wrong I had done, then God would reward me accordingly with a fullness of joy and a fruitfulness in ministry that would impress everyone in the denomination in which I served.

He didn't.

And I couldn't understand why.

Others who in my judgment were not as sincere, nor as dedicated, nor as diligent, were experiencing blessing in their ministries, and that offended me. One of the ladies who attended our church but had some habits I judged as unholy and unbecoming to a believer visited a sister church of our denomination in Pretoria and had a powerful encounter with the Holy Spirit—truly a "fatted calf" experience where the Father showered her with kisses, gifts, and a feast with music and dancing.

I couldn't join in the celebration. Instead I stood outside the party, complaining to God, "What about *me?* Where is *my* skinny goat?"

Just weeks before her experience, I had spent an entire night on my face on the carpet of the church where I pastored, only to rise totally exhausted and completely frustrated at God's apparent unwillingness to bless me as I cried out to him for his touch on my life. Privately, I felt that her experience could not be from God because it had not changed her "unholy habits," nor made her regular in her church attendance. I could thoroughly understand the older brother's anger in seeing the father bless someone who had not been as diligent and devoted as he and leave him unrewarded for all his diligent service and perfect obedience.

My problem?

I focused on the reward I thought I deserved. And only on the reward. When I didn't get it, I felt slighted. And when someone less deserving got it instead, I sulked.

—

As I studied in that trailer, I saw that the difference between the mentality of the servant and the son had a lot to do with the difference between the mentality of a believer living under the old covenant and a believer living under the new. It became apparent to me that I was a new-covenant believer living under the inferior motivations and mind-set of the old covenant.

My study of the Last Supper proved to be a turning point. I realized in my studies that I had overlooked the significance of this Passover meal as a great divide that separated the old covenant from the new. I knew that Jesus' death, burial, and resurrection was a watershed in revelation of the fulfillment of the old and the ushering in of the new. But I had failed to see the striking contrasts that Jesus drew on the occasion of that meal. I failed to understand that the Passover meal, representing the old covenant, was being superseded by another meal, announcing a new covenant.

The instituting of a new covenant meant that the whole basis for relating to God was changing. Jesus, in his post-meal discourse, announced the many changes that were being initiated through the meal and what it portrayed. Prayer, for example, was moved into a new dimension of asking in Jesus' name (see John 16:24) and being assured that God, as our Father, would give us whatever we asked for in that name!

The intercovenantal transition can be found in John 15:15: "No longer do I call you servants, for a servant does not know what his master is doing; but I have called you friends, for all things that I heard from My Father I have made known to you." The word *friend* that Jesus uses here is a covenant word. Abraham was called God's friend because of God's covenant with him. Jesus was identifying a dramatic change in the relationship between the disciples and God, something that was happening at that very moment.

No master takes his servant into his confidence and shares the deep secrets of his heart with him. Such familiarity would breed contempt and destroy the formality necessary to maintain authority. Note Solomon's warning in Proverbs 29:21 against raising a servant in familiarity: "He who pampers his servant from childhood / Will have him as a son in the end." Jesus' implication in John 15:15 was that the master only communicated to his servant the information he needed to fulfill his responsibility and no more. That communication consisted primarily of commandments for the servant to obey. The master was not obligated to tell the servant why he should do what the master desired. The servant did not know what his master's purpose was, didn't know what his motivation was, and didn't know what his overall plan was. The servant only knew the assignments for that day's work.

It is tragic that so many Christians see themselves as servants rather than sons, their communication with God limited to finding out only what God wants them to do. They never feel comfortable claiming his promises except on the condition of their obedience. Neither do they expect God to reveal the deep secrets of his heart to them.

Such thinking reveals a basic misunderstanding of the covenant meal. The Old Testament antecedent for the bread in the New Testament meal is the showbread, or, literally, the "bread of his face" (see Ex. 25:30). Remember in 1 Samuel 21:6 how Ahimelech gave David the only bread that was available, the showbread, "which had been taken from before the LORD." The showbread represented unrestricted, uninterrupted, face-to-face communion with God. When the elders of Israel ascended Mount Sinai with Moses and Aaron, "they saw God, and they ate and drank" (Ex. 24:11).

Just as Jesus was revealed to the two Emmaus Road travelers

in the breaking of the bread, so the bread of the new covenant meal guarantees the unveiling of the face of God to the believer. He wants to be intimate with us and can be intimate since we are no longer servants.

Jesus then declared us to be on a par with him as far as revelation from the Father is concerned: "All things that I heard . . . I have made known to you" (John 15:15).

At the same time, Jesus was introducing the disciples to his successor, the Holy Spirit—whom he called "the Spirit of truth" (John 14:17)—who would teach them all things (see 14:26) and guide them into all truth (see 16:13). "He will take of what is Mine and declare it to you," Jesus stated (John 16:14). He then interpreted what his use of the word *Mine* entailed: "All things that the Father has are Mine" (John 16:15).

Nowhere in the old covenant do we hear such extravagant promises—the promise of an intimate form of communication, the promise of a personal form of guidance, the promise of a share in the things that the Father has given to his dearly beloved son.

Is it difficult to believe all this is for you without you having to do something to deserve it? If so, you're not alone. The son in the parable of the prodigal son felt that way too. And I'm not talking about the one who left home. I'm talking about the one who stayed.

—

In a later chapter I want to go over the gifts that the father lavished upon the younger son. But here I want to talk about the meal the father prepared upon his return. After the errant son was welcomed home and showered with gifts and affection, the father called for the fatted calf to be killed (see Luke 15:23).

We are now coming to the heart of the story and the heart of the difference between a servant and a son. The father had ordered the fatted calf killed to celebrate the younger brother's return. In all probability, the older brother himself had been entrusted with the special care of this calf. Day after day he had diligently given it the extra nutrition to fatten it up. He had possibly daydreamed of the celebration when, in recognition of his exemplary behavior, his father would give him that very calf for a feast with his friends.

If we listen closely to the text, the resentment of the older son comes through clearly: "Yet you never gave me a young goat, that I might make merry with my friends" (Luke 15:29).

The Greek word here for "goat" is *eriphon*. Some manuscripts use the diminutive form of the word: *eriphion*. The word literally means "tiny goat" or "skinny goat." I believe the latter translation better reflects the sarcasm of the older brother. The comparison is so obvious! The father killed the fatted calf for his younger brother but had never even given him so much as a tiny, skinny goat. How insensitive! How unfair!

Here is the classic dilemma of the legalist who cannot grasp the superiority of mercy over justice. Jesus had told the Pharisees: "Go and learn what this means, 'I desire mercy and not sacrifice'" (Matt. 9: 13). In the Pharisees' minds, there was no way that mercy was superior to sacrifice. James, in summarizing his discourse on partiality and judgmentalism, declared: "For judgment is without mercy to the one who has shown no mercy. Mercy triumphs over judgment" (2:13). This last phrase can best be translated: "Mercy is superior to justice."

The audience that first heard the parable of the prodigal son was composed of legalists. The preoccupation of legalists was the minutiae of the law. They noted and footnoted every requirement. Every detail. Every jot and tittle. The Pharisees and scribes were so intent on doing everything the law demanded that they completely overlooked the true nature of God. They related to him based on their performance. If they fulfilled all the requirements, then God, they reasoned, would reward them accordingly.

Here are some of the characteristics of a legalist:

- A legalist is one who lives his life regulated by laws and rules.
- A legalist's goal is flawless compliance with every rule he believes applicable.

42

- A legalist believes that acceptance by God is dependent upon perfect conformity to all the laws, ordinances, and precepts laid out in the Bible.
- A legalist is hard on himself but at the same time covers his failure to live up to the standard he sets himself with a hypocritical outward show of piety.
- A legalist compares his performance to that of others around him and is either puffed up with pride because he sees himself as better than others or else is driven to despair because he sees others as better than himself.
- A legalist is extremely judgmental of others around him, for in finding fault with them he feels better about himself and his own performance.
- The hope of a legalist in his life of rigid discipline, self-denial, and perfectionism is to earn a reward from God.
- When God fails to reward a legalist according to his expectation, and when he perceives God acting unfairly toward those he considers undeserving, he is angry and offended.

The older brother, with his servant mentality, portrayed many of these characteristics. His blindness to the true nature of his father distorted his relationship with his father. He was oblivious to all the benefits of living in his father's house. Only one thing consumed him: his reward! Having served the father so diligently and having obeyed him so perfectly, he felt sure the father would reward him accordingly. Instead, when the father blessed the younger brother, the older brother became confused, frustrated, and angered.

It was customary in New Testament times for the estate of a father to be divided on an unequal basis. The older brother, being the firstborn son, would have received a double portion of the inheritance. The younger brother would have received a third part of the father's estate—that which he squandered. However, in reinstating the younger brother to his position as a son, the father now entitled him to a third part of the remaining estate. We can see how obviously this would have added to the older brother's anger.

I recently heard a similar story of a businessman who had brought his older son into the family business. This son, through hard work and astute business dealings, had helped the father build the family business into a multimillion-dollar empire. The youngest son had never been interested in the family business and had gone his own way to sow his wild oats. After many years of irresponsible, reckless living, and alienation from the family, a radical change happened in his life, leading to reconciliation and restoration with his father. The father, overjoyed at the return of his prodigal, proceeded to bring him into the business as a full partner with his hard-working brother.

You can imagine the reaction! Suddenly the offended older brother had to deal with all sorts of emotions as he attempted to handle on one hand his father's extravagant generosity, and on the other hand the lack of appreciation for his faithfulness, stability, and diligence.

Now we come to the crux of the servant-son dilemma. At issue is the skinny goat. Why did the father not reward the older brother for his long years of diligent service? The answer to that question contains one of the most important truths you will read in this book: it was impossible for the father to reward the son with that which already belonged to him by inheritance!

All the skinny goats and fatted calves *already* belonged to the older son, for when the father gave the younger son his inheritance, the older son had received his also: "So he divided to *them* his livelihood" (Luke 15:12, emphasis mine). Every single calf and goat already belonged to him! He could have had a party every day of his life. The father said to him: "All that I have is yours" (Luke 15:31).

What a tragedy! Since the older brother perceived himself as a servant rather than a son, he awaited a reward and forfeited the enjoyment of his inheritance. Everything his father had was his by inheritance, but he was never able to receive what was rightfully his to enjoy. His servant mentality limited him to the anticipation of a wage or reward and kept him from recognizing his liberty as an heir to appropriate what was his.

Why do Christians who earnestly desire everything that God has for them never receive the blessings promised to them?

The answer is clear: they await a reward for their service, and, because they are heirs, the Father can never give them as a reward what belongs to them as a birthright.

Dear Father,

I confess to you my legalism.
Forgive me for not seeing it as the sin that it is—
    the insidious, self-satisfied sin that has kept me so far from you;
      so far from your house,
        and all its fullness;
      so far from your heart,
        and all its goodness.
Forgive me for living in the age of the new covenant
    and acting as if I were living in the old,
      with its inferior mind-set of
        seeing rewards in the Christian life
      as wages that are due me,
        rather than gifts that are given me.
Forgive me for grumbling when you celebrate someone else.
Forgive me for standing out in the field of my self-righteousness,
    complaining about how generous you are with others
      and how stingy you are with me.
Come out to get me, Lord, bad attitude and all, ugly words and all.
Come out to talk with me, to reason with me,
    to put your arm around me
      and walk me home.

The Living Quarters
of the Servant

CHAPTER FOUR

But you received the Spirit of adoption by whom we cry out, "Abba, Father."

Romans 8:15

Years ago, my wife and I traveled to Kyrgyzstan, staying in the city of Bishkek for a three-day conference with Kyrgyz pastors and leaders from around the nation who had gathered there. All weekend I poured into them the message of the Father's love—the love that had made us sons and given us a place of honor rather than of servitude.

It was our first visit to Kyrgyzstan, and we were thrilled to see the eagerness with which these leaders received what to them was a new message. What I was preaching was in sharp contrast to the messages of service, commitment, obedience, performance, and discipline they were accustomed to hearing from visiting preachers from the United States.

I spoke about the difference between a servant and a son. I highlighted the temporary nature of the relationship of the servant to the master and how it was performance based. The servant performed his duties and then retired to the servant's quarters to await the dawn of another day to perform yet another list of tasks set by the master. However, I told them, after the servant left the master's house, the son remained there, spending the evening enjoying a sweet time with his family.

As I spoke, I noticed a smile on the face of one of the pastors in the meeting. Sergei was of Russian descent and worked part time in security at the American Embassy in Bishkek. He was well dressed, obviously more affluent than most of the pastors there. As I ended my talk, Sergei excitedly came to me.

"I know exactly what you are talking about," he said. "My wife's family owns a farm where we grow carnations and other flowers in large, temperature-controlled hothouses. Each day we cut and pack blooms to ship overnight to cities in Europe and Asia. The laborers on the farm are a grumbling bunch of malcontents. They are always complaining and trying to get away with as little work as possible. At the end of the day, they collect their pay, go to their quarters, drink vodka, and complain about the work and their employers. When they leave, the family gathers in the family farmhouse to enjoy a relaxed meal together and talk over plans for expansion, dream of future prosperity, and plan vacation trips together to enjoy the wealth that our family enterprise brings us."

Stop a moment and think about all that is offered you as a son or daughter, living in your father's house, enjoying all that Jesus enjoyed when he walked this earth—the same intimacy he had with the Father, the same guidance he had from the Holy Spirit, the same things he shared with the Father.

Imagine that.

Imagine *all* of that.

Now imagine turning your back on it. Turning your back and walking away. Shuffling off to the servants' quarters when a room in the Father's house is being offered you, along with everything that comes with it—the intimacies, the teaching, the guiding, the gifts. All that—the hopes; the dreams; the joy of each other's company; the sharing of thoughts, plans, feelings—is shared around the table, all while the house is filled with music and feasting and dancing.

I can't imagine anyone in the world who would walk away from that.

Yet for so many years I did. For so many long and weary years. Perhaps you did too. Perhaps you are still doing it. Are you tired of living that way? Tired of living in the servants' quarters, serving a to-do list, living in fear, insecurity, and condemnation? You don't have to stay there. You can move out. Out of the servants' quarters and into the Father's house.

How?

It begins with a word.

———

Jesus taught that living as a servant leaves us with a sense of incompleteness and with a fear that we have not done enough. The law, he told us, is a merciless slave driver. It is never satisfied. Even our best efforts fall short of the perfection it demands. If we revert to trying to please God through obedience to the demands of the law, the fear that we're not good enough will be the result, and we will "again" receive the "spirit of bondage" (Rom. 8:15). In contrast to that, Paul affirmed the truth of what happens when we become children of God: "But you received the Spirit of adoption by whom we cry out, 'Abba, Father'" (Rom. 8:15)!

Paul's words are so rich that I want you to savor every word. The first word I want to linger over is "Abba." It is an Aramaic word that is equivalent to our modern-day *Daddy*. It implies familiarity and intimacy. When I first brought our family to the United States in 1982, I was amazed at the formality with which many children addressed their parents—"Yes, sir" to their fathers; "No, ma'am" to their mothers. I felt good about Tracy and Brad addressing other adults that way, but not addressing Bev and me that way. After all, we were their parents, not their masters. And they were our children, not our servants. As our children, they have a special relationship with us—special access to us that the neighbor children don't have, special privileges that even the children of our extended family don't have, and a special closeness that no one in the world has.

"Adoption" is the second word I want to pause over. The Greek word literally means "the placing as a son." Our placement into the family of God, which is more than simply a legal adoption, is accomplished by God's Spirit through the new birth. When we were placed into the family, we not only received the nature of the Father and the Spirit of the Father, we also received all the rights of a legal heir, including inheritance rights!

"We cry out" is the next part of the verse I want you to consider. Awakened by the grace of God moving over it, the Spirit within us is stirred to cry out in faith, "Daddy, Papa, Abba, Father!" An interesting cross-reference to this verse is Galatians 4:6, where Paul said that "the Spirit" cries out. I believe that is what Paul is implying in Romans 8:16: "The Spirit Himself bears witness with our spirit that we are children of God." The word translated *with* means "alongside," as in a duet. We cry out; he cries out. When you, in simple faith, begin to cry out in

53

confession that God is now your Daddy, the Holy Spirit comes alongside your spirit and echoes into the depths of your soul his cry, "Daddy! Abba! Father!"

Looking deeper into the cross-reference, we see that this Spirit is "the Spirit of His Son" (Gal. 4:6). The Spirit, whom God sends to indwell us, is the same Spirit who dwelled in Jesus! Why would we ever fear rejection by God when the Spirit within us is the same Spirit who lived within Jesus? Why would we ever think that we need a labyrinthine maze of commandments to lead us in the paths of righteousness when the Spirit indwelling us is the same Spirit who caused Jesus to perfectly please the Father? Our reverting to living by rules and regulations is an insult to grace and to the goodness of the Father's heart from which that grace originated.

The next word I want to look at in the Galatians passage is "cry." No timidity and tentativeness here! This strong crying is based on strong conviction. You might start a little timidly and feel embarrassed at the thought of calling God your Daddy! But as you begin, the echo of his Spirit will resound within you. As a result, you will gain confidence, momentum, and volume until you are literally crying out! Never fear expressing your emotions in the Father's presence. Jesus didn't. Remember how he prayed in the Garden of Gethsemane? With "vehement cries and tears" (Heb. 5:7). So shout it loud, shout it long! *"Daddy, Abba, Father!"*

The assurance of your sonship through the reverberating witness of the Holy Spirit begins with confession. If you keep saying you are just a servant, you will never break out of living in the servants' quarters. But if you confess the truth of your identity through the new covenant, you will move into the Father's house and into the liberating joy of being his son or daughter.

It is likely that many of you reading this book are on a treadmill of performance, filled with rejection, feeling hopeless. You've hit a wall. And no matter what you do, you can't break through to the assurance of your sonship. Here is God's solution: get off the treadmill. Your salvation came through faith, not works. Why would you think that your assurance comes any differently? If you are waiting for God to come to you personally and give you some kind of subjective experience of assurance, you may have a long wait.

He has already come to you . . . in the person of his Son.

Now it's your turn . . . to come to him.

Here's what I suggest: Find a place where you will not be disturbed or cause a disturbance. By faith, cry out the truth that you are a son or a daughter. He is your Father. You have a God-given right to come boldly into his presence and cry out.

First, repent of the words of your mouth that have contradicted the revelation of the purpose of Jesus' work on the cross. He did not come to redeem servants. He came to bring "sons to glory" (Heb. 2: 10). You are not a servant! You are a son! You are a daughter!

Now, begin to cry out: "Abba!" "Father!" "Papa!"

I know what you're thinking, know what you're asking yourself. I know because I once thought the same things, asked the same questions.

Who in the world could believe such things? you're asking. *They seem so simple, so—what's the word?—so make-believe,* you're thinking.

Who could believe that a faraway God who dwells in regal splendor—an almighty God who created the heavens and the earth—who could believe that such a God wants a relationship with you and with me? Wants to be with you and with me? Wants to dine with us, live with us, share his life with us, his future with us, his fortune with us?

I know what you're thinking.

It's too much of a fairy tale to take seriously.

Yet I'm asking you to take it seriously, asking you to believe what seems make-believe, asking you to live a new life, to begin again.

Moving out of the servants' quarters into the Father's house begins with a word.

Abba.

A simple word. Spoken from simple lips.

A child's lips.

Abba, Father . . .

I am so tired,

> so very, very tired.

I'm tired of performing, tired of serving a to-do list,

> tired of making my list and checking my list,

> > tired of showing my list to others to impress them,

> > > tired of praying my list to you to impress you.

I want another life,

> a new life.

I want out of the servants' quarters.

I want to come home.

Please, Papa.

Sit me on your lap,

> hug me,

> > still me.

Love on me, Abba.

Sit with me and just love on me.

I am so tired,

> so very, very tired.

PART II

THE FATHER

THE PICTURE OF
THE FATHER

CHAPTER FIVE

It does not, therefore, depend on man's desire or effort, but on God's mercy.

Romans 9:16 (NIV)

B eginning in 2000, Bev and I lived in South Africa for a period of eighteen months. It brought back a lot of wonderful memories as we returned to live in a friend's beach house a few miles from the Igoda River, where God had met me so powerfully in 1982. Bev's mother, our last surviving parent, was in poor health in a retirement home, and Bev would spend her time tending to her mother's needs, enjoying a depth of relationship she had not experienced during her childhood.

My reason for going there was to write a book on the new

covenant. But day after day, as I sat at my computer, attempting to write, nothing came. Since the writing was going so poorly, one day I busied myself with tidying up the storage area in the administrative offices of the church. The offices were located in the house that had been our home during the years Daddy pastored the same church. This was the same house that held so many of my painful childhood memories—the "left behind" memory, my worst whipping of my life that I got when I was twelve, the continual confrontations over tasks I hadn't done.

In that storeroom, I found a pile of photographs of the men who had served as pastors of that church. My daddy's picture was on top, the frame now broken, the backing loose, and the matting around the picture faded in the forty years since the photograph had been taken.

As I held that photograph, a riptide of emotions washed over me—love for the good man Daddy was, sadness over the lack of intimacy in our relationship, regret for the harsh words I had said in my last visit with him before his death in 1974. The argument had been a theological one, where I challenged his view of sanctification. How often I wished I could take back those words. If I had known how few words we had left to say to each other, how different the conversation would have been.

As I held his washed-out picture in my hands, I thought to myself, *I am going to restore Daddy's picture.*

Immediately the Holy Spirit spoke to my heart, saying, *That is what I am doing. I am restoring Daddy's picture.*

The impact of those words could not have been greater had Gabriel appeared to hand deliver them! Suddenly I realized: the picture I had of my heavenly Father had been distorted by the picture I had of my earthly father. That picture started to change in my trailer by the river on January 8, 1982. I have already described the scene of Jacob at the Jabbok River on January 7, where I expressed my desperation for God to meet me and change me. The next day, my journal reflected the sudden parting of the clouds of despair, where the sunshine of divine revelation showed me the Father's true nature. I remember the moment with great clarity. I was reading Romans 9. The first verse I jotted in my journal was 16: *"It does not, therefore, depend on man's desire or effort, but on God's mercy"* (NIV).

I underscored the last two words with a red pen.

"God's mercy."

As I read further, I found myself identifying with the people of Israel, who, like the older brother in the parable, tried to pursue righteousness under the law through their works. On the other hand, the Gentiles, like the younger brother, found mercy, receiving the gift of righteousness without even pursuing it!

How unfair that seems to the perfectionist, the legalist, and the Pharisee.

That is precisely why the older brother couldn't come into his father's house and join the party. It all seemed so unfair. And that is precisely why *I* couldn't come in and join the party. How unfair of God to lavish his love on those who didn't deserve it.

But that is the point of grace—the whole point. It is a gift that is given, not a wage that is earned. Righteousness is not remuneration for work well done. It doesn't come through human desire, human effort, or human accomplishment. It doesn't come through the merit of mankind but through the mercy of God. We don't become righteous by the law; we become righteous by grace. Not by works but by faith.

My meditation in Romans 8 was followed by Galatians 3: "Did you receive the Spirit by observing the law, or by believing what you heard? Are you so foolish? After beginning with the Spirit, are you now trying to attain your goal by human effort?" (vv. 2–3 NIV)

How could I have missed that? And how could I have missed it for so long?

No wonder God never answered my prayers to bless me. I was expecting a reward based on how diligently I had served and how perfectly I had obeyed. It was about me. It was *all* about me. *My* desire. *My* effort. *My* keeping the letter of the law, down to the smallest jot and tittle. I had "human effort" in spades.

I was looking for compensation. When I didn't get it, I acted like a disgruntled employee who had been shortchanged on his paycheck. *It wasn't fair,* I grumbled in the small-claims court that my heart had become. *I showed up every day for work, put in my time, did my job. And for what? For not so much as a skinny goat.*

As I read, it seemed as if Paul was preaching directly to me. He was saying, in essence, that the gifts of God, which are the birthright blessings to his sons and daughters, can only be received by believing. Paul was insistent. It's not about our performance; it's about God's promise.

My picture of God was so distorted. I saw him as a judge. But, I was beginning to realize, if God *is* our judge, as he was under the old covenant, we would have to observe the law in order to obtai   we are not under the old coven   relates to us now is as a father.   he wants us to hear and beli   teed us in the new covenant thr

Why was i   promises? I began to see that it   od. The Hebrew word for "kn   ge, not intellectual knowledge. I   am knew Eve his wife, and she   her? Intimately. The same wo   David declares:

You have searched me and known me.
You know my sitting down and my rising up;
    You understand my thought afar off.
You comprehend my path and my lying down,
    And are acquainted with all my ways.
For there is not a word on my tongue,
    But behold, O LORD, You know it altogether. (vv. 1–4)

I had known God, but I hadn't *really* known him. Why? Because everything I had believed about him was based on a distorted picture. And that distorted picture distorted everything. It distorted how I read the Bible, how I prayed, how I preached, how I related to my family, how I related to the members of my church. It distorted how I saw everything. Even how I saw myself.

My picture of God was not the picture that Jesus gave us. My picture was formed by my daddy's picture. Daddy was a good man, but I never knew at what moment my behavior would cause him to erupt in anger and whip me. How could you draw near to such a father? How could you trust him? How could I be sure that some act of disobedience on my part might not cause him to withhold his blessing or unleash his wrath?

Like the Pharisees, my distorted picture of God made me leery of Jesus' picture of God. How could a holy God tolerate the debauched character of those who flocked to him, ate with him, drank with him? Surely if Jesus was from God, he would have had nothing to do with those who were spiritually bankrupt. Instead, he would have denounced their sin with fiery words of divine censure. How could he receive sinners and eat with them (see Luke 15:2) and still maintain that he had been sent from God?

My journey of having my father's picture restored has led to an amazing unfolding of the true nature of the Father. That journey was given a dramatic forward push in 1989, as I was captured by Paul's ranking of a good man above a righteous man in Romans 5:7. What did he mean when he said that almost no one would give their lives for a righteous man, although some might be willing to make the supreme sacrifice for a good man?

I believe that when Paul spoke about a righteous man, he was thinking of someone who was intent on doing everything right, following all the rules and never messing up. Such people tend to be perfectionistic and are uncomfortable to be around. You feel measured, weighed in the balance, and found wanting. When you are around them, you feel as if a makeup mirror has been held to your face, making every flaw glaringly visible to all.

In contrast, a good person is so full of kindness that you

feel comfortable and accepted in his or her company. Someone like that is not trying to expose your weaknesses. That person's generosity of spirit makes even flawed people relax and feel at home.

Aha! I was discovering something so amazingly wonderful! *That* is why tax collectors, harlots, and sinners loved to be around Jesus and were so relaxed that they reclined with him at the dinner table. It was his genuine goodness and unreserved kindness that set them at ease.

Take Zacchaeus, for example. Jesus chose to visit with this corrupt, hated tax collector. The goodness in Jesus' spirit created a comfortable, safe environment in which, though there was no pressure to change, Zacchaeus found himself wanting to and choosing to change. The goodness of God expressed in Jesus produced a true repentance.

As I studied the goodness of God, I was amazed at how I had missed such a thoroughly biblical concept for so long. I discovered that the essence of the glory of God is not in his omniscience, not in his omnipotence, not in his omnipresence. The essence of his glory is his goodness. "Please, show me Your glory," requested Moses. And God responded: "I will make all My *goodness* pass before you" (Ex. 33:18–19, emphasis mine).

Jesus' entire life was one, long, streaming video that displayed the goodness of the Father. Peter, who had the privilege of up-close observation of the conduct of Jesus, summarized his entire ministry when he said: "[He] went about doing good . . . for God was with Him" (Acts 10:38).

How had the Pharisees—or, to make it painfully personal, how had *I*—missed what was so obvious in the Scriptures? King David continually extolled God's goodness and mercy, but all I could see was his harshness and his justice. All I saw was a judge with a quick gavel and a reputation for handing out the stiffest of sentences.

What a distorted picture I had.

What kind of picture do you have?

Whatever it is, it is likely influenced by the picture you have of your own father. If he was aloof, likely your picture of God as a father is an aloof one. If your father was authoritarian, likely your picture is an authoritarian one. If your father was abusive, likely that has influenced in some way the picture you have of your heavenly Father. Was your father angry? If so, how has that influenced your picture of God? If your earthly father was absent, how has that distorted the picture you have of your Father who is in heaven?

Our Father, who art in heaven . . .

How beautiful those words sound when I say them.
Our *Father!*
Affectionate, loving, compassionate, good.
Our Father!
You are ours, which also means you are mine!
Forever you are mine, Lord, and *forever* I am yours.
How wonderful *those* words sound when I say them,
      how absolutely, incredibly, unbelievably wonderful!
Thank you for all the pictures of you
      that Jesus left behind—
            pictures of your goodness,
               your kindness,
                  your mercy.
Use those pictures, Father, to restore the faded ones,
      the bent ones, the torn ones, the distorted ones,
            so I might see you for who you are,
               know you for who you are,
                  love you for who you are.

And use those same pictures to restore the distorted pictures
    I have of myself,
        so I might see myself for who I am,
            know myself for who I am,
                love myself for who I am.
Which is yours!
Forever and always . . . *yours!*

THE ACCEPTANCE OF THE FATHER

CHAPTER SIX

And the Pharisees and scribes complained, saying, "This Man receives sinners and eats with them."

Luke 15:2

And he arose and came to his father. But when he was still a great way off, his father saw him and had compassion, and ran and fell on his neck and kissed him. And the son said to him, "Father, I have sinned against heaven and in your sight, and am no longer worthy to be called your son." But the father said to his servants, "Bring out the best robe and put it on him, and put a ring on his hand and sandals on his feet. And bring the fatted calf here and kill it, and let us eat and be merry; for this my son was dead and is alive again; he was lost and is found." And they began to be merry.

Luke 15:20–24

Where are you?" came a voice in the garden.

Can that be the voice of God, thought Adam, hiding among the trees? *No, it's impossible. He wouldn't come to me now, not after what we have done.*

"Where are you?" the voice called again.

Adam timidly emerged from hiding. "I heard your voice . . ."

"Who told you that you were naked?"

Although Adam and Eve hid from God, God did not hide from them. The separation did not come from God's side. It came from man's. God was still reaching out to them, to fellowship with them. It was their guilt and shame that created the barrier.

The Pharisees and scribes, together with a large percentage of Christians today, were scandalized by the thought that the holy God revealed in the law of Moses could have any association with sinners. Wasn't God of purer eyes than to behold evil (see Hab. 1:13)? How then did God come to seek out Adam (see Gen. 3:9), to walk with Enoch (see Gen. 5:22), to share a meal with Abraham (Gen. 18:1–8), to save Noah and his family from the flood (see Gen. 6:17–18)?

It was grace!

Everything changed, though, when the law was given. God withdrew his presence from free association with sinful man to dwell behind a curtain in Moses' tabernacle. His heart longed for the freedom to have personal relationships with his creation, but the law restricted him to only be approached by a high priest once a year with an atoning sacrifice. Occasionally, though, God would give Israel an inkling of a plan he had prepared before he created the world.

When King David brought the ark back to Israel after its capture by the Philistines and after it languished in Kirjath Jearim for twenty years, God instructed him not to put the ark of the covenant of Moses back in the tabernacle of Moses (see 2 Chron. 1:3–4, cf. 29:25). Instead David pitched a new tent for it in Jerusalem in which free access was available to everyone to the presence of God—so much so that even Obed-Edom, who came from the same city (Gath in Philistia) as the giant Goliath, was named a doorkeeper in David's tabernacle (see 1 Chron. 16:38).

Although it was completely contrary to the law given through Moses, God loved it. He loved it so much that he promised through Amos that he would restore the tabernacle of David "so that the rest of mankind may seek the Lord, and all the Gentiles who are called by My name" (Acts 15:17 NASB, cf. Amos 9:11–12). He wanted all people to have free access to him. It was this prophetic promise spoken by Amos that was quoted by the apostle James at the council in Jerusalem in Acts 15, silencing the Pharisees who had become believers but still felt that the Gentiles needed to be circumcised and "to keep the law of Moses" (v. 5).

God never wanted to treat people as enemies. He wanted to treat them as friends, hoping they would trust him. It was only when Israel refused to trust him that God added the law (see Gal 3:19). But that addition, said Paul, could not subtract from the covenant or promise given to Abraham (see Gal 3:17). God had always wanted man to come to him in simple trust as a child to its Father.

Enter Jesus. Full of grace and truth. Full of love and kindness. And, dare we say it, full of fun. No wonder the tax collectors and sinners loved him! Jesus loved them, accepted them, and, to the horror of the religious establishment, enjoyed their company. He was the fulfillment of Amos's prophecy. He was the tabernacle of David (see John 1:14), the place where God meets "the rest of mankind" (Acts 15:17). He was God living in a human tent, totally approachable to the vilest sinner. Totally accepting of the worst offender (see John 8:10–11).

For much of my life I was a slave to the law. Without realizing it, I had mixed aspects of the old covenant with the new, blurring the distinction between law and grace. Ironically, it was the law, not my sin, that had separated me from a warm and intimate relationship with the Father. But that didn't keep God from seeking me, finding me, changing me. I changed when my understanding of the new covenant changed. The parable of the prodigal son was pivotal in that process.

In Luke 15, the covenantal aspects of the father's love to his returning son illustrate the wonderful liberty that comes to a repentant child returning to God for forgiveness and restoration. I believe the items of dress summoned by the father, as well as the killing of the fatted calf for a feast of celebration, have covenantal significance. In the making of covenants, there would be an exchange of gifts (often items of personal clothing such as a valuable robe or a ring), the slaughtering of an animal, or the shedding of blood by the parties involved, and the sitting down to a feast to celebrate the making of covenant. Just as in the cutting of the Abrahamic covenant recorded in Genesis 15, where God's covenant making was unilateral (he waited until Abraham was overcome with exhaustion and fell asleep), so here, because the son was regarded by the father as being "dead" (v.24), the action of the father was unilateral. The son could do nothing but receive, in childlike faith, the father's magnanimous gesture of restorative love.

As the son began the speech that he had prepared, the father interrupted him by calling out to the servants: "Bring out the best robe and put it on him, and put a ring on his hand and sandals on his feet. And bring the fatted calf here and kill it, and let us eat and be merry" (Luke 15:22–23).

The father did not expect his son to do anything to make himself ready to reenter the father's house. He commanded the servants to bring out the best robe, the ring, the sandals, and the fatted calf to where they were. The son had to go no further in the state in which he had returned. What a wonderful picture of our Father's gracious love that unconditionally comes to where we are and changes us. He takes the initiative to change us and forestalls any attempt at self-improvement in order to come into the Father's house. We come just as we are. As we do, he lavishes us with gifts.

Let's take a closer look at the gifts the father gave his errant son. Each reflects an aspect of the father's covenantal love.

The Robe

The description in the Greek is "the robe, the best (or first) one." This would not be just any garment. A robe was used as formal wear as opposed to daily attire. The "first" or "best" one would indicate a robe reserved for very special occasions such as festivals and birthdays.

The robe has a twofold meaning in covenant making.

First, the robe symbolizes life. An exchange of robes signifies the willingness of the two parties to lay down their lives for each other. An illustration of this can be found in the case of Jonathan and David (see 1 Sam. 18:4). Here, however, there was no exchange to one another. Certainly the son's dirty, smelly garment that represented his old life was removed from him to make way for the best robe and so reminds us of the reclothing of Joshua the high priest in Zechariah 3:4. The father was giving the returning son his own life as a gift. He was received back, not with the life he once lived (of which he was now ashamed and from which he was turning), but with a new life imparted to him—the father's own life.

Second, the robe represents possessions. In covenantal terms, the one giving the robe was saying, "Everything I have now belongs to you. Whatever you may need, if I have it, it is yours. If ever you are in a situation of lack, all that I have is at your disposal. As long as I have possessions, you will never be in need." Though the son had taken his inheritance and squandered it, and so had no legal claim to anything the father owned, the father was committing to his son not a portion but all that he had.

The Ring

The ring the father called for is a wonderful picture of restored authority. The son had forfeited his position as a son, and therefore his authority. The signet ring of the father placed on the son's finger would boldly declare the son's restored position as a member of the family, for that signet ring would carry the family seal. The gift of the ring was another covenant act of exchange. The son's forfeited rights were replaced by the imparted rights, not merely of a son but of the father's own authority.

The Sandals

The sandals are a symbol of the son's restored position. He had not been received back as a servant, but as a son. It was customary for slaves to go about their duties barefoot as a symbol of their subservience. The servants were instructed to place the robe, ring, and sandals on the returning son, indicating their subordinate position to him. The sandals given to the son were a mark of honor, a daily reminder that the father had not acquiesced to the son's desire to be hired as a servant, but had restored him to the position of a son.

The Fatted Calf

Now that the gifts have been given, the father called for the fatted calf to be killed so that by the shedding of blood, the covenant might be sealed and the celebratory feast prepared. The calf had been separated from the herd and given special food in order to prepare it for some unique occasion of celebration. In the father's mind, no greater opportunity for celebration could be found that would warrant the slaying of the special animal.

His son was dead but now was alive. He was lost but now was found. What cause for joyous celebration with feasting and dancing! "Bring the fatted calf here!" he called. He wanted it slaughtered at the very spot in the road where he had embraced the returning son. In the pouring out of the calf's blood on the spot that marked such an emotional restoration, a life was being given so that, figuratively, from the blood-drenched dust there might emerge a new life for his son.

—

Child of God, it is time for you to be confronted with the position to which the Father has restored you. We have for too long been deceived by mixing the old covenant with the new. But I believe that as you have read this chapter, there has been a quickening in your heart as the implications of the father's restoration of the prodigal son begin to resonate in your spirit.

Please realize:

You are received unconditionally, just as you are.

Think back to the moment when you came to God as a sinner and invited Jesus into your heart. Like the prodigal son, you came and were received just as you were. You were not expected to change yourself as a prerequisite to being received into the Father's house. Like the prodigal son, when you came to the Father, he was waiting for you, not with words of condemnation but with words of welcome. With merciful eyes, he had been watching for you. With a merciful heart, he ran to you. With merciful arms, he embraced you. And with merciful lips, he kissed you with a kiss of forgiveness and grace. What love! No probationary period was prescribed for proving yourself truly repentant. No "cooling-off" period was required where the Father could work his way back to not feeling angry at you for your rebellious and sinful behavior. No! You were received with a genuine and wholehearted display of love, grace, and mercy.

You are given a robe of righteousness, life, and inheritance.

The Father placed on you the robe of his righteousness. You never sit feasting at the Father's table in the robes of your own righteousness. However beautiful they might appear to you, before him they are but filthy rags. He has stripped those garments from you and replaced them with the gorgeous robe of his perfect righteousness. The reason that you are so freely received at the Father's table is that whenever he looks at you, he sees you covered with the robe of his own righteousness that has been given to you through your faith in Jesus Christ. The gift of righteousness has now fitted you to stand unintimidated and uncondemned before the Father. It is a gift of life. You were once dead, but now you are alive! And there is more: that robe, representing all that the Father has, marks you as an heir. All that the Father has is now yours!

You have been given the ring of authority and dominion.

Through Adam's sin, man forfeited his position of dominion and authority in this world. Through Christ, the Anointed One, however, dominion and authority have been restored to us, not only over all the works of God's hands, but also over the one who usurped that authority—Satan, together with all of his demonic hosts. It is for this very reason that Satan does not want you to ever lose your sense of unworthiness and guilt. As long as you feel condemned and unworthy, you will never be a match for his powerful deception and intimidation. He knows exactly what button to push to vanquish a self-conscious Christian from the fight.

You have been given the sandals of honor.

The cumulative evidence of the Scriptures that we have studied thus far is presented to settle forever in your spirit that you are not a servant but a son or a daughter of God. It is hardly likely that the prodigal son could ever overlook the significance of the robe and the ring. However, should he do so, there would always be the impact of the distinctive sandals that, every time he placed them on his feet, would remind him his father had ignored his proposal to be made a servant and had marked him in this conspicuous fashion as a son.

As a child of God, you have been marked by the Father with the gift of distinctive sandals. "Stand therefore . . . having shod your feet with the preparation of the gospel of peace" (Eph. 6: 14–15). They are the sandals that provide a "firm footing" (the word translated as *preparation* in the New King James version of the Bible carries this meaning) given by the gospel of peace. What is your confidence and "firm footing" as a child of God? What gives you the right to walk confidently into the presence of the Father without any fear of rejection? It is simply this: "Therefore, having been justified by faith, we have peace with God through our Lord Jesus Christ, through whom also we have access by faith into this grace in which we stand, and rejoice in hope of the glory of God" (Rom. 5: 1–2).

You have been declared righteous by the One who has the right to condemn you to death. In an act of sheer grace, he has accepted the sacrifice of Jesus on your behalf and now sees you as righteous. Look down at your sandals! They will declare the truth to you that you need to hear today. The good news is that there is peace in your relationship with God. He is no longer antagonistic toward you. He has been reconciled to you and has already reconciled you to himself in Jesus Christ (see 2 Cor. 5:18–19). "Since Christ's blood has now given us God's approval, we are even more certain that Christ will save us from God's anger" (Rom. 5:9 GOD'S WORD). Good news! God isn't mad at you! Receive that truth today. By faith, step over into the firm footing of grace! Rejoice! You are accepted! You are forgiven! You are loved!

Welcome, "Son"!

Welcome, "Daughter"!

Welcome home.

Dear Father in heaven,

Who sought out Adam and Eve in their hiding,

who sought out Abraham in the land of his ancestors,

who sought out David in the fields as he tended his sheep,

who sought out sinners and tax collectors,

who left the ninety-nine and sought the one
that was lost,

who sought out me in my lostness,

in my aloneness,

in my hiding and in my cringing.

You sought me and found me,

forgave me and restored me,

not as one of your servants but as one of your sons.

Thank you, Father.

Thanks for running to me as I crested the hill.

Thanks for the hugs, the kisses, and the tears.

Thanks for the robe of righteousness, the ring of authority,

the sandals of honor.

And for the party! How fun it was!

Help me to lavish on others what you so freely have lavished on me,

giving them a heartfelt welcome when I see them,

an open-armed embrace, the biggest of smiles,

and the best of celebrations.

THE JOY OF THE FATHER

CHAPTER SEVEN

The Son of man came feasting, and you say, "Here is a lover of food and wine, a friend of tax-farmers and sinners."

Luke 7:34 (BBE)

E dith Schaeffer, in her book *A Way of Seeing*, talks about what has happened with the word *father* over the centuries by people who turn from God because of painful memories they've collected from their earthly fathers. "It is all backwards when a torn pattern—a spoiled pattern— is followed and handed down year after year, and people forget what the original pattern was like."[1]

That is what happened with the Pharisees in the first century. They viewed God as distant, unapproachable, harsh, and humorless. They had it all backward. Year after year they followed a distorted picture that had been handed down to them, forgetting what the original picture looked like. Schaeffer goes on to restore that picture for us.

> A father should be the first one a child would think of communicating with when overwhelmed by physical woes, psychological problems, confusing philosophies, conflicting ideas as to what to do next. A father is meant to be a shelter. A shelter shuts out wind, rain, ice, cold, heat, sand, pursuing mosquitoes, or armies of men. A father is meant to be a strong tower of protection. The very word *father* should conjure up a feeling of safety and security. The shelter of God the Father shuts out dangers but also shuts one in to the realities of fulfillment. The fulfillment pictured by a family around a fireside—communicating and sharing ideas as well as experiences in an atmosphere of warmth and caring—is meant to picture in a minimal way the perfection of God's fatherliness in being ready to listen and advise, give counsel and guidance. "In His presence is fullness of joy."[2]

In his presence is fullness of joy.

When you think of your earthly father's presence, do the words "fullness of joy" come to mind? How about when you think of your heavenly Father? If they don't, you have a distorted picture of him—a "torn pattern," to use Edith Schaeffer's words. One of the reasons Jesus came to this earth was to restore that torn photograph to its original condition.

One of the ways he did that was by example. The apostle John said, "No one has seen God at any time. The only begotten Son, who is in the bosom of the Father, He has declared Him" (1:18, cf. Heb.1:1–3). Everywhere Jesus went he left behind pictures of the Father. Pictures of his goodness. Pictures of his compassion. Pictures of his joy. When the Pharisees followed him, they couldn't make sense of the pictures. Jesus was eating and drinking with the most questionable company. And if that wasn't bad enough, he seemed to be enjoying their company. "A lover of food and wine, a friend of tax-farmers and sinners" is the way Luke records their reaction (7:34 BBE).

What can you expect from a man who started his public ministry turning water into wine? Imagine producing 150 gallons of the best wine for a wedding celebration where the guests were probably well on their way to intoxication. Some have been so scandalized by that behavior that great pains have been taken to distort the clarity of the language of Scripture and explain that the wine was unfermented. In that case, the attendees would not have been commenting to the organizer of the feast about keeping the best wine till last, but for foisting on the revelers some inferior drink when they were too inebriated to know the difference.

Why did Jesus commit such a serious error of judgment in using his miracle-working power to produce such an abundance of wine to further intoxicate a celebratory crowd? What was Jesus revealing in all of this misunderstood behavior?

The fullness of the Father's joy.

The joy of giving triggered the Father's compassion in Jesus and moved him to miraculously relieve an awkward situation and provide a superabundant, undeserved gift that brought joy to the guests and relief to the organizer. What mercy! What kindness! What a lavish gift!

Jesus said that if you have seen him, you have seen the Father (see John 14:9). Being in the presence of Jesus was like being in the presence of the Father. Full of the same grace, the same truth, the same compassion. And full of the same joy.

The other way Jesus helped to restore distorted photographs of the Father was by parable. Luke 15 is a case in point. What prompted the parable was the Pharisees grumbling at Jesus' association with sinners—eating with them, drinking with them, enjoying himself a little too much. Eating too much. Drinking too much. Laughing too much.

It was scandalous. Had Jesus no sense of propriety? No sense of decorum? No sensitivity to what people thought, what they said? How offensive! How brash! What kind of example was he setting? The grumbling got louder and more strident.

In response to their criticism, Jesus told three stories: one about finding a lost sheep; another about finding a lost coin; and the final, climactic one about finding a lost son. What each one had in common was joy.

"Rejoice with me" to celebrate my finding the lost sheep (v. 6).

"Rejoice with me" to celebrate my finding the lost coin (v. 9).

And finally, to celebrate finding the lost son:

> "Bring the fatted calf here and kill it, and let us eat and be merry; for this my son was dead and is alive again; he was lost and is found." And they began to be merry. Now his older son was in the field. And as he came and drew near to the house, he heard music and dancing. (vv. 23–25)

The Pharisees and scribes, like the older brother, could not understand the Father's joy. A feast? With tax collectors? Music and dancing? With sinners? With a hedonistic son? What kind of precedent was that setting? What would people think?

Jesus didn't care what people thought. He cared about what his Father thought. And he cared about clearing up any misunderstandings about who he was. For he knew a misunderstood God leads to a misguided faith.

Proof of that can be seen in the familiar picture of the church at Laodicea, scrapbooked with pictures of other churches in Revelation 2 and 3. The church in Laodicea was a hypocritical church. They pretended to have it all together. But Jesus could see past the pretense, assessing them as "wretched, miserable, poor, blind, and naked" (Rev 3:17). The picture that Jesus presented to them places him outside the door of the church, patiently knocking and waiting for someone to open the door.

We must ask the question: why would a church that was in such a pathetic state keep Jesus on the outside? The answer has to be that they were afraid of what he might do if ever they invited him in.

I confess that I understand their reluctance. And their fear. My daddy had a burning passion to see revival come to the various churches that he served. I can remember the monthly, all-night Friday prayer meetings in the church in Port Elizabeth. When I wasn't sleeping under the pew on the floor, I must say that the prayers ascending heavenward, begging God to come and expose the wickedness of our hearts, terrified me. I felt I could do without that. I don't think I ever purposely prayed against such a revival coming, but I was relieved after those prayer times that nothing seemed to happen.

You see, the picture that the old covenant presented was that the day of the Lord was a bleak day, a terrifying day, a day of visitation and of judgment. John the Baptist thundered about the fiery judgment that would burn the chaff with unquenchable fire (see Luke 3:17).

Then Jesus showed up. And John found himself confused, even offended. He sent disciples to inquire, "Are you the Coming One, or do we look for another?" (Luke 7:20). How could John have doubted that Jesus was the Coming One when he had seen the heavens open and the Holy Spirit coming down and settling on him? God had told John that was the sign by which he would recognize the Son of God (see John 1:32–34). So why was he doubting?

There was no fire and brimstone, there was no setting the sociopolitical and religious systems of the day in order, there was no censure of the wickedness of men's hearts. Where was the unquenchable fire that John had prophesied, burning off the chaff?

Could this really be the Messiah? How could he be? thought John. He didn't fit the picture. Instead he healed all who came to him, never inquiring as to their spiritual state.

No doubt the Laodicean church was petrified that if ever Jesus showed up, they would be exposed as hypocrites and humiliated. Now, here stood Jesus knocking at their door.

What would your reaction be?

Religion tells us that first we must get our house in order. Repent or else!

But what does Jesus say? He says to whoever hears his knock and opens the door: "I will come in to him and dine with him, and he with Me" (Rev 3:20). In other words, "Let's have a feast!"

But what about the wretchedness, the moral poverty, the spiritual blindness? What about the house being a moral mess with everything in disarray? Would Jesus not feel more comfortable if he first cleaned house and then sat down to eat?

The pattern of Jesus' life on earth gives insight into God's method of transformation. He knows that you, like Zacchaeus, will not be changed by performance but by his presence. The power of his love, the joy of his presence, and the peace coming from his acceptance are far more capable of changing the human heart than rebuke, censure, condemnation, and rejection.

As Edith Schaeffer said: "The word *father* should bring thoughts of one who is full of marvelous plans for the joy of his children—little joys day by day: the lunch together, the walk in the woods together, the game together, the book enjoyed together, as well as plans for longer periods of fulfillment ahead."[3]

Those are the pictures of the Father that Jesus left behind.

Beautiful, aren't they?

The only thing that would make them more beautiful would be if you were in them! I don't know where you are in your relationship with God, but I do know this: he loves your company, wants you to feel relaxed in his presence, just as the tax collectors and sinners felt as they reclined with Jesus, eating with him, drinking with him, laughing with him.

Answer the knock on the door, won't you?

Let him come in.

And let the celebration begin!

Thank you, Father,

For sending Jesus to restore the pictures of you
        that have been handed down from one generation to another,
                washed-out and worn, bent and torn.
Thank you for how beautifully he lived his life,
        leaving behind such winsome pictures,
                full of grace and truth,
                        full of love and compassion,
                            full of joy.
I want to be a part of that party, Lord,
        part of the celebration of the lost and found.
I want you to come in and dine with me.
I want to be in your presence, Lord,
        and *stay* in your presence,
                because in your presence is the fullness of joy.

PART III

THE SON

THE POSITION OF THE SON

CHAPTER EIGHT

And he said to him, "Son, you are always with me, *and all that I have is yours."*

Luke 15:31a (emphasis mine)

It is mind-boggling to imagine how much the older brother forfeited as a result of his servant mentality. Think of all the times he could have taken a calf from his daddy's herd and had the servants prepare a feast for him and his friends. Think of the joy he could have experienced in drawing close to his daddy, working with him, talking with him, eating with him. Think of the love, the favor, the generosity he could have enjoyed.

Those were all the son's rights by birth.

The most powerful statement about the birthright is made in the passage: "Son, you are always with me, and all that I have is yours" (Luke 15:31). Here the father states the two fundamental birthrights of every believer: intimacy and inheritance. The one has to do with our position; the other, with our possessions. In this chapter we will focus on the first of those rights—our position as sons.

In addressing the older brother as "son," Jesus did not use the usual Greek word *huios*. Rather he used the word *teknon*. The change is significant. Had he used the word *huios*, Jesus would have been emphasizing the nature of the relationship between the father and his son. The word is used for an adopted son, for example. In every other place where "son" is used in this story, this is the Greek word that is used.

So why does Jesus change the word?

The word *teknon* is derived from the word *tik*, which means "to beget, bring forth, or bear" a child. By using the word here, the father was drawing attention away from the nature of the relationship to the foundation upon which the relationship was based. The father saw him as a son, not because of the son's behavior but because of his birth.

You and I are not children of God because of our service; we are children of God because of his seed. "Whoever has been born of God does not sin, for His seed [Greek *sperma*] remains in him" (1 John 3:9), "having been born again, not of corruptible seed but incorruptible, through the word of God which lives and abides forever" (1 Peter 1:23). "But as many as received Him, to them He gave the right to become children of God, to those who believe in His name: who were born, not of blood [natural birth], nor of the will of the flesh [human initiative] . . . but of God" (John 1:12–13).

Like the son in the story, our position as a son does not come through doing; it comes through being. And our being comes through birth. We were born from his "seed," which is his Word. Someone once said that an acorn holds within itself an entire forest. So it is with our spiritual seed. You and I have our Father's nature and character because his seed *remains* in us. Because it remains in us, it grows in us, and is genetically coded to mature in us. Our potential is determined by our position.

When the father said, "Son, you are always with me," he made the most sublime statement about our position. The words "with me" stress presence; the word "always" stresses permanence. Our birthright from him is a continual intimacy with him. That is something he doesn't offer strangers, neighbors, even friends. He offers them access but not intimacy. Look closely into Jesus' parable on prayer in Luke 11 and see if you can distinguish the positional difference in the relationships.

Which of you shall have a friend, and go to him at midnight and say to him, "Friend, lend me three loaves;

for a friend of mine has come to me on his journey, and I have nothing to set before him"; and he will answer from within and say, "Do not trouble me; the door is now shut, and my children are with me in bed; I cannot rise and give to you"? I say to you, though he will not rise and give to him because he is his friend, yet because of his persistence he will rise and give him as many as he needs. (vv. 5–8)

The meaning of the parable is nestled next to the father. Do you see it? "Do not trouble me; the door is now shut, *and my children are with me in bed*" (emphasis mine). The picture is of the warmth, closeness, and intimacy that is ours within the father's house. If the man reluctantly answers the request of his friend on the outside, how much more eagerly will he answer the request of his children on the inside? The friend standing at the door has to knock; the children lying next to him in bed have only to whisper. The one has to persist; the other has only to tug on his nightshirt.

Here is the point: we are not the friend on the outside; we are the children on the inside. Lying next to him. Snuggled warmly by his side. He is that near to us.

And we are that dear to him.

—

The Pharisees and scribes claimed to be the ones who had the true knowledge of God. Through this account of the older brother and his reaction—both to his brother's return and to his father's reception—Jesus was revealing their ignorance of God as a father. In doing so, he was also revealing their ignorance of themselves as sons.

Seeing themselves in the story must have been sobering, for they were the critical older brother, ignorant of their own father's heart.

How could they be so ignorant?

After all, they were experts in the law. Through the law, God was revealed as demanding and austere, one who could not tolerate failure and disobedience. His holiness was revealed as being unable to have any contact with sinful, unbelieving man. But that was not the complete revelation of God in the Word. Under that same law, his mercy provided a sacrificial system that foreshadowed a perfect, redemptive sacrifice to open the way into his presence. The prophets foretold a new covenant that God would make, mercifully allowing mankind to draw near to God.

The religious leaders, who should have understood this, were unable to grasp not only God's tolerance for sinners, but also his acceptance that permitted intimate fellowship with them. Instead of being delighted by Jesus' display of the Father's love, they were incensed.

Jesus came into the world to reveal the Father and to clear up any false perceptions of him. Jesus himself said, "He who has seen Me has seen the Father" (John 14:9). The testimony of Hebrews 1:3 confirms this: "[Jesus] being the brightness of His glory and the express image of His person." In spite of this, many still live with a false dichotomy between the Father whom Jesus revealed and the God whom the law revealed. Many Christians still differentiate between a holy God who is so pure that he cannot look upon sin and Jesus, who is so permissive that he ate with sinners. The only way the two pictures can be reconciled is through the new covenant that enables even the most sinful to come home and be restored to their position as sons.

May I talk with you a moment about your own perception of God?

The Father loves you, receives you, and wants to have intimate communion with you. He desires to break through whatever distortions you have of him so he can show you his love and his goodness. Do not let the story of the older brother become your story. How sad to have lived under the father's roof for so many years and yet never really have known him. How sad to have gone to church all your life, knowing all the hymns but not knowing *him*.

I spent a lot of years like that. A lot of years standing out in the fields, serving a Father I hardly knew. Serving and stewing. Like the older brother in the field. Like Martha in the kitchen.

Until one month in a trailer changed that.

After that month, I felt no more condemnation, guilt, and fear. No more wondering if God was mad at me for something I had done or failed to do. No more waking up every day to a to-do list of tasks to keep God off my back. No more going to sleep at night apologizing for another list of failures and unfinished tasks.

The joy of understanding my position as my Father's son came to a glorious pinnacle toward the end of my month in that trailer at Igoda. I drove into East London to spend time in prayer with a pastor friend. In that time of prayer, at long last, I was able to receive the Father's gift of the Holy Spirit as an inherited gift rather than as a reward. That evening, rather than returning to Igoda, I decided to stay in the city with Bev and the children. The children had turned in early. Bev had taken her bath and gone to bed too. I came into our bedroom and was overwhelmed with a desire to pray. As Bev lay in bed, I knelt next to her and began to pray.

Even now as I write, I can clearly recall the excitement I felt as I prayed. It was as though I were listening to another person praying. For the very first time in my life I felt as though I was right in the Father's presence. No longer did I feel like a stepchild in the family. No longer did I feel like an outsider, longingly looking into a picture of true family intimacy that was reserved for others. There was such a sense of closeness and communion as words of adoration poured from my heart through my lips to God. I felt like one of his children, lying next to him in his bed, curled up to the warmth of his love.

Never had I experienced prayer like this. Prayer had always been a discipline, a chore, a duty, a means of gaining God's approval. Now it was a delight to be in my Father's presence and talk to him so intimately, as though he was right there with me. No longer was there a distance between us.

I have never been the same since.

And I have never had a moment's doubt of my position as a son.

It is hard for me to exaggerate the dynamic change in my emotions. Having lived under a spirit of condemnation—with its accompanying feelings of unworthiness, abandonment, and frustration—for so long, the emotional joy and peace of feeling loved and accepted was indescribably wonderful. In the years since then, that joy has never decreased. Rather, as I have gained more insight into the new covenant, there has been a steady intensification of what I felt that night . . . realizing that I was no longer a servant but a son.

I want to conclude this chapter with an e-mail that a man wrote me after he read an earlier version of this book that I had self published:

Dear John,

Where to begin? A close friend gave me the name of your book. I went online, ordered it and read it twice. He then gave me three CDs with teaching by you. I feel as though a bomb has gone off inside of me. Everything is different now, my perspective, my peace, my joy, my hope, and my appetite for spiritual things. My world has been rocked. You see, I've been saved for 31 years. I'm a husband of 21 years, father of two, businessman, and worship leader/teacher. My life in general has been externally very blessed, but frankly quite miserable. I lived hidden, defeated, condemned, shamed, guilty . . . you name it . . .

I read your book and immediately began to listen to your teaching on covenant.

John, this is the message I have longed for my entire life. If I was indeed saved initially, it was a peripheral blessing to the greatness of the New Covenant . . . I never thought the gospel was such great news. Yes, I was saved, but when I finally faced God would He really be pleased with me, would His acceptance of me be with reluctance because of my poor performance as a Christian? I just could not lift my head with confidence.

I understood your message right away. I have never heard ANYONE teach it, however. But I intuitively knew it to be true, instantly. I actually arrived at many of the same conclusions regarding the law and the Church turning the New Testament into the law. I also knew that it could not be both ways. Yet no one else was present to confirm my convictions, and, in fact, I was told it was bordering on heresy to think that the New Covenant didn't have a large portion of righteousness by works attached to it. It truly is too good to be true. But it is. I've found the gospel to truly be good and wonderful news. I'm on my eleventh time of listening to the New Covenant teaching. Something happens inside me every time I listen . . .

For me I feel like I heard the true gospel for the first time . . .

Transformed,

Greg[1]

Did you see yourself anywhere in the e-mail? Has your life in general "been externally very blessed, but frankly quite miserable"? Do you live "hidden, defeated, condemned, shamed, guilty"?

If so, I hope these truths will rock your world the way they rocked Greg's.

And that it will feel like you're hearing the true gospel for the first time.

Dear Father,

Thank you that I am not the friend standing on the outside,
   but one of the children sleeping on the inside.
Next to you.
Close enough that I can feel the warmth of your goodness,
   touching the softness of your nightshirt,
      as I tug at you with my prayers.
Thank you that you are that near to me,
   and that I am that dear to you.
Thank you for my birthright, Lord,
      for the intimacy and the inheritance and all that is mine
         because I am yours.
All because I am yours.

THE POSSESSIONS
OF THE SON

CHAPTER NINE

And he said to him, "Son, you are always with me, and all that I have is yours."

Luke 15:31 (emphasis mine)

We have already seen why the son could not receive what was rightfully his. His servant mentality was the barrier to him receiving it. In the same way, so many of God's children are unable to receive what is rightfully theirs by covenant.

Mephibosheth, an Old Testament character, best illustrates this. Mephibosheth was the son of Jonathan and the grandson of King Saul. Since a covenant had been made between David and Jonathan, Mephibosheth was the heir of the covenant promises made by David to his beloved friend.

111

There came a day when David summoned Mephibosheth to his palace and fulfilled his covenantal obligation: "Do not fear, for I will surely show you kindness for Jonathan your father's sake, and will restore to you all the land of Saul your grandfather; and you shall eat bread at my table continually" (2 Sam. 9:7).

Notice the parallel between David's declaration and that of the father in the two stories we are studying. Both are a promise of intimacy and inheritance, of position and possessions. Mephibosheth was to eat bread at David's table "continually." That parallels the father's words: "You are always with me" (Luke 15:31). David restored to Mephibosheth all the land that had belonged to his grandfather, and the father said, "all that I have is yours." The son's birthright was the same as Mephibosheth's covenant rights.

But the story of Mephibosheth doesn't end there. Although he was received as an heir and enriched by David through the covenant made with his father, Jonathan, and although he sat in the king's palace among David's sons, enjoying the bounty of David's table, he couldn't escape the shame caused by his crippled condition. He never stopped seeing himself as a worthless, undeserving "dead dog" (2 Sam. 9:8). That pitiful self-image was the very thing that caused him to ultimately forfeit his inheritance.

You see, Mephibosheth had a lying, scheming enemy named Ziba who was apparently consumed with anger and jealousy toward him. Until David restored the land to Mephibosheth, Ziba—who had been Saul's servant—had treated the land as his own (see 2 Sam. 16:1–4, 19:24–30). He was obviously consumed with the desire to get the land back for himself.

The climax to the story is tragic, yet so representative of many of God's children. When David decided to split the land between Mephibosheth and Ziba, Mephibosheth—in an act that I used to consider one of humility—said, "Rather, let him take it all, inasmuch as my lord the king has come back in peace to his own house" (2 Sam. 19:30).

It sounds very spiritual for someone to say, "If all I have is Jesus, that is all I need. My kids might be on drugs, my marriage falling apart, but as long as I have Jesus, I am happy."

What is wrong with such thinking? This type of thinking negates the fact that the birthright of the son is not just intimacy but also his inheritance. Mephibosheth's covenant right was to possess his father's inheritance. He forfeited his rights because he was ignorant of the covenant and because of his sense of his own unworthiness.

It is obvious from what he said that he was looking at himself as the grounds for David's blessing. He never once acknowledged that he was blessed for Jonathan's sake. He did not understand his acceptance and endowment on the basis of covenant. Therefore, since he saw no value in himself, he was ready to forfeit his entire inheritance that was secured for him by his father in the covenant made with David.

In preaching on Mephibosheth, I love to ask an audience the question: "What should Mephibosheth have done when David was splitting his inheritance between him and Ziba?" Think about it for a moment.

What *should* he have done?

There are many things that he could have done but, really, there was only one thing he needed to say: "Jonathan! Jonathan! Jonathan!"

The mention of that name would have stopped David in his tracks, and he would have remembered his precious friend whom he loved so deeply. He would have thought back to the two occasions when, because of their love for each other, they had made a covenant together. He would have remembered the promises he had made to Jonathan and would immediately have reversed his decision.

We, too, have an enemy. His name is Satan. He, too, has stolen what does not rightfully belong to him. God gave it to Adam and Eve and their offspring. But similar to Ziba, Satan usurped that which God had placed under man's feet and over which he had given him dominion.

The only way you can resist the devil is by knowing your rights as a son or daughter and standing firmly on them. That will involve the confession of your mouth. You will need to declare the covenant promises of God to you, and you will need to declare them repeatedly and authoritatively.

Satan does not want to give up the possessions he has stolen from us and the dominion he has usurped from us. The Bible instructs us: "Resist him, steadfast in the faith" (1 Pet. 5:9). To resist the devil means to stand firm against him. The word *steadfast* means "firm" or "hard." What is called for is an unyielding and unwavering stance in faith. Faith is of no benefit in resisting the devil if it remains silent. My faith in the Word must become verbal and vocal. We must "hold fast the confession [literally "saying the same word"] of our hope without wavering" (Heb. 10:23).

The devil will use intimidation, weariness, discouragement, and disappointment to stop our confession of what God has said. We, like Mephibosheth, have a name that unlocks the treasure chest of the wealth that is ours by covenant. You can readily understand why the enemy tries to keep our focus on ourselves. As long as we are coming to God based on who we are in ourselves and what we have done, we will slink out of his presence, crawling out in shame and unworthiness. But when we grasp that our rights and privileges are in the name of the one who made covenant with God the Father on our behalf, we will come boldly and expectantly, speaking the name: "Jesus! Jesus! Jesus!"

Begin now to confess what Jesus declared to us in the parable: "All that I have is yours." Say right now: "All that the Father has is mine!" The enemy may come and intimidate you by saying something like, "Who do you think you are? What right do *you* have to come to God? Look at your life. Look at your shameful, crippled life. How can someone like *you* dare to ask for such things from God?"

If the enemy comes accusing you like that, resist him by bolding declaring, "All that the Father has is mine, in the name of Jesus!"

Say it, and don't stop saying it until Satan flees with his accusations and the Spirit returns with his assurances (see Rom. 8:16).

—

In Galatians 4:7, Paul said: "Therefore you are no longer a slave but a son, and if a son, then an heir of God through Christ." Reading the New Testament is like reading the last will and testament of a wealthy benefactor, where the riches of his estate are enumerated. Here is what is bequeathed us. We are:

- heirs of eternal life (Matt. 19:29)
- heirs of salvation (Heb. 1:14)
- heirs of the promise (Heb. 6:17)
- heirs of the kingdom (James 2:5)
- heirs of the grace of life (1 Peter 3:7)

- heirs of the blessing (1 Peter 3:9)
- heirs of all things (Rev. 21:7)

And that is the short list.

Here is the full accounting of the assets:

- The estate of a king has been willed to us.
- We are heirs of *all* that belongs to the Father.
- By right of birth, *every* spiritual blessing is ours.

Imagine that for a moment. Imagine having resources like that to draw upon. Now imagine how secure you would feel if you believed that. I mean, *really* believed that.

Sadly, many of God's children don't believe that. And because they don't, they live like paupers with regard to the riches that have been willed them.

Why?

One reason is ignorance. We, like Mephibosheth, don't know what is ours. The good news is our inheritance is a matter of public record. All we have to do is search the Scriptures. God doesn't want to keep our inheritance a secret. It is not locked up in some executor's safe. He wants us to know what all he has for us. In 1 Corinthians 2:12 Paul told us: "Now we have received, not the spirit of the world, but the Spirit who is from God, that we might *know* the things that have been *freely* given to us by God" (emphasis mine).

Another reason is unworthiness. We, again like Mephibosheth, feel unqualified to sit at the table of the king and to partake in the inheritance that is ours by covenant. We feel we don't deserve it, that we are not good enough, not qualified enough. Again, it is not our performance that qualifies us; it is our paternity, as Paul told us in Colossians 1:12, "giving thanks to the Father who has qualified us to be partakers in the inheritance of the saints in the light."

Don't let anyone tell you that you have been somehow cut out of your Father's will, or for some reason have been disinherited. Don't let some moral failure in your life wag an accusatory finger at you, telling you that you do not qualify. Don't let a low self-image shame you into thinking that you don't qualify. And don't let the enemy—the accuser of the brethren—tell you that, either.

The *Father* has qualified you.

The new covenant is the Father's last will and testament, so to speak, sealed by the blood of his very own son. That covenant changed how he relates to us and how we relate to him. No longer do we relate to him as servants; now we relate to him as sons.

One of the great misconceptions among Christians is that Jesus' teaching of the servant-master relationship in his parables is applicable for today. Because of a lack of understanding of the purpose of his teaching during his earthly ministry and the transition marked by the institution of this covenant meal, people live under a burden of performance that was terminated through the cross.

If that is true, it begs the question: what was Jesus' purpose in teaching so extensively on the requirements of the law? He had come, he said, to uphold the law in order to ultimately fulfill it. In light of this, he was inflexible in teaching the stringent requirements of the law. This was preparatory to his glorious work of nailing the "handwriting of requirements that was against us" to the cross (Col. 2:14). Having instituted the covenant meal and having introduced his disciples to the "new covenant in My blood" (Luke 22:20), Jesus declared the transition in their relationship from servant-master to one of covenant friendship. As friends, they were now in a position to possess as their very own whatever he had received from the Father.

The new covenant is not between God on the one hand and us on the other. If that were the case, the promises and blessings of the covenant would be dependent upon our fully satisfying all of God's righteous requirements to keep the covenant in force. They would no longer be a promised gift appropriated through faith, but instead an earned reward for our obedience to the law.

The wonder of the new covenant is that God cut a covenant with himself! He became man in his son, Jesus Christ. Then, as man, he fully satisfied his own demands for righteousness, shed his own blood as a sacrifice for man's failure to live up to those righteous demands, and by that same blood he cut a covenant with himself on man's behalf. The perfect God-man could perfectly represent God to man and man to God. Only by Jesus being fully God and fully man could we be assured that what he did on our behalf was acceptable to God.

Now, through the new birth, we are united with Christ in that sacrificial death and are raised with him to enter into the enjoyment of communion with God and participation in the Son's inheritance of all that belonged to the Father. By that same death and birth we have died to the law and been born into a new relationship with Christ, which Paul describes as a marriage (see Rom. 7:4). The law has no jurisdiction or influence on a dead man. Instead, by his union with Christ, he now lives in the freedom of no longer being under law but under grace (see Rom. 6:14).

In Christ we are in covenant with God.

In Christ we become his children and therefore his heirs.

Paul gave us a magnificent insight into God's purpose for his children in Ephesians 1:3–5: "Blessed be the God and Father of our Lord Jesus Christ, who has blessed us with every spiritual blessing in the heavenly places in Christ . . . having predestined us to adoption as sons by Jesus Christ to Himself, according to the good pleasure of His will." God has not predestined us to an assignment as servants with the nebulous hope of a wage, but to "adoption as sons," and with that adoption comes the inheritance of "every spiritual blessing."

Note Paul said that God has *already* blessed us. The inheritance is already ours. So many Christians have never entered into the full enjoyment and appropriation of their inheritance. What is keeping them from it?

Part of the reason why Christians have never lived off their inheritance is that they are ignorant of the promises that are ours as beneficiaries. One way I have addressed that problem is through Communion. Since the Holy Spirit opened my understanding to the wonderful truths of the new covenant, one of the beautiful things that has developed is my understanding of Communion. As a child growing up, I hated Communion because it seemed so morbidly introspective as we were told to "examine ourselves" to see if there was any unconfessed sin. I had plenty, but I felt hopeless then about ever getting free from them, regardless how often I confessed them.

Now I understand Communion more as a covenant meal where we have the wonderful privilege of remembering all the covenantal promises the Father has made to us and confirmed to us by Christ's death. Now when I lead a congregation or groups of people in celebrating this joyful event, I love to give everyone the opportunity to recite a promise of God that they are believing him for. When the person finishes, the rest of the congregation answers "Amen."

What promise are *you* believing God for? I believe it would help you if you put that promise on paper:

_____

_____

_____

_____

In answering, think biblically. But also think big. For an inheritance of staggering proportions is ours. Come boldly to the throne of grace, the way the young officer did in the following story.

The great French conqueror, Napoleon, in his quest to rule the world, was quite surprised on one occasion when he encountered unexpected resistance while attempting to capture an island in the Mediterranean. The fighting was fierce, and he lost many good men in the battle before finally overcoming the enemy.

Napoleon and his generals were having a celebration feast when from out of nowhere, it seemed, a young officer approached him. Napoleon saw the young man and asked abruptly, "What do you want?"

The young man said, "Sir, please give me this island."

The generals were deeply offended at the brashness of the young man. But, suddenly, Napoleon asked for pen and ink, promptly writing out a deed to the island. He then signed it and gave it to the impetuous officer.

By this time the generals were astounded. They asked their leader, "How could you give away this island to that young man when so many of our men paid such a high price to obtain it?"

Napoleon responded, "He honored me by the magnitude of his request."

My daddy often quoted the words from the hymn "Come, My Soul, Thy Suit Prepare" written by John Newton (author of the famous hymn "Amazing Grace"):

> Thou art coming to a King,
> Large petitions with thee bring;
> For His grace and power are such,
> None can ever ask too much.[1]

Dear Father in heaven,

Please send your Spirit to come alongside me as I read my Bible,
> to enlighten my eyes to all you have so freely given me.

How can I be grateful if I don't know what I have been given?

And I want to live a grateful life, Lord.

I want to give thanks for every blessing, every promise, every gift
> that you have given me.

I don't want even one to remain unopened.

Because if it is unopened, it is unknown.

And if it is unknown, it will be unappreciated.

And if it is unappreciated, it will be unused.

If unused, then I am the poorer,
> those around me are the poorer,
>> and the world is the poorer.

Which is tragic in light of how much wealth has been entrusted me.

Forgive me, Lord, for the many ways I have
> squandered my inheritance,
>> not so much by wasting my inheritance the way
>>> the prodigal son did,
>>> but by not even knowing what was there to waste.

Especially I ask forgiveness for . . .

PART IV

THE FATHER'S HOUSE

The Journey to the Father's House

CHAPTER TEN

Then when he came to himself, he said, How many hired servants of my father have enough food, and [even food] to spare, but I am perishing (dying) here of hunger! I will get up and go to my father, and I will say to him, Father, I have sinned against heaven and in your sight. I am no longer worthy to be called your son; [just] make me like one of your hired servants. So he got up and came to his [own] father.

Luke 15:17–20a (AMP)

J esus did not give a conclusive ending to this story; he left it at the point where the older brother was still angry while the party continued to celebrate the return of the prodigal. I would, however, like to add an ending of my own. It is speculative and uninspired, but it is, nevertheless, a tragically accurate commentary on so many Christians. Bear with me as I tell my tale.

The festivities have ended, and the servants are engaged in the cleanup of the dining area. The father sits in his favorite chair. On the one hand he is happy to have his younger son back, but, on the other, he is troubled by the obstinance of his older son. The father is lost in thought as he reviews the events of the day. Suddenly he realizes that he has not seen his younger son for a while. He wonders, *Where could he be?*

He beckons one of the head servants and asks him, "Have you seen my young son anywhere?"

"Yes, sir," replies the servant. "I saw him going out the back door."

The father hurries out the door, making his way down the path, where he meets another servant, going about his duties.

"Have you seen my young boy?" asks the father.

"Yes, sir," replies the servant. "I saw him entering one of the rooms in the servants' quarters."

The father quickens his pace. He enters the servants' compound and finds the room where his young son is.

"Son, what are you doing here?"

"Preparing a place for myself for the night."

"Come back to the house, back to your room. It's waiting for you."

The young son averts his eyes from his father's gaze. "Father, you don't know all the things I did in the far country. I am so ashamed to have brought such dishonor to your name. I feel too unworthy to sleep under the same roof."

"Son," replies the father, "don't you understand? When I called for the servants to place on you the best robe, I was covering all of your old life with the gift of a new life."

"But, Father," the son insists, "your goodness in receiving me back is the very thing that makes what I did in the far country seem so terrible. The shame I feel over the life that I lived makes it impossible for me to accept a position as a son. I am completely happy to be a servant."

"No, son," the father responds, "that can never be! If you continue to think of yourself as a servant you would be totally misunderstanding what I have done in receiving you home as a son."

"How could I possibly have any expectations beyond a wage since I have already squandered my inheritance? I came home to be a servant, and that is what I intend to be for the rest of my days."

Exasperated over his son's inability to grasp the significance of his gracious act, the father responds, "Son, do you not understand that when I gave you my robe, it was a guarantee that everything I have belongs to you?"

"No, Father, I have no right whatsoever to expect anything more than a servant's position and wage."

"Son, look at the ring on your finger and the sandals on your feet. What do they tell you? It is true that you have forfeited your rights as a son. However, when I placed that ring on your finger, I was giving you my own authority. I gave you the right to the benefits and blessings of being a son and an heir."

The guilt the son feels and the memories he carries have so blinded him that he can see neither the father's mercy nor the grace that has been extended him.

"Come home to where you belong, son," the father begs.

"No, Father; that can never be. I will stay here."

Dejected, the father turns and leaves, returning to his house. Though he often tries to reach his son, no amount of reasoning can convince the young man of the significance of what the father did in that amazing moment when he ran to him, threw his arms about him, and kissed him. For the rest of his days, the father grieves over both of his sons for never coming to understand his merciful generosity.

Sadly, the ending is not happy. Both sons continue to serve him faithfully, but both neglect their true inheritance of entering into a deep relationship of loving intimacy with their father.

—

Instead of allowing God to write a happy ending to their own stories, many Christians are writing a tragic ending because they just do not grasp the Father's mercy and grace. Why is this happening in so many believers' lives?

The problem is this: we are unable to see ourselves as God sees us. We are so self-consciousness; the recorded memories of the past and the misunderstanding of the gospel combine to blind our eyes to the truth. We cannot escape the accusatory voice that convinces us of our unworthiness and condemns us to the position of a servant for the rest of our lives.

It is imperative that we allow the truth of God's Word to challenge the lies of Satan who uses our history against us.

"Behold the Lamb," John the Baptist declared when Jesus appeared at the Jordan (John 1:29). What did that mean? In Moses' tabernacle, a sin-burdened worshiper approached the priest with a suitable sacrifice for his sin. The priest would then examine the animal to be sure the sacrifice was unblemished. If the animal was without a spot or blemish, the worshiper was accepted into the presence of God.

Not once did the priest examine the worshiper! *Not once!* It was not about the unblemished condition of the worshiper. It was about the lamb.

Behold the Lamb!

It is the Lamb who is without blemish and God has accepted Him in our place. Why would we then look at our state as the basis for acceptance?

Behold the Lamb!

Let me ask you: where is your focus? The Lamb or yourself? When you come into God's presence do you immediately find yourself making a list of the things that disqualify you or are you coming into his presence through the Lamb?

The desperate need of the Church is for repentance, not from being in the far country and the pig pen, but from living in the servants' quarters. The older brother desperately needed a change of mind from his servant mentality to the reality of being a son. The younger brother needed to repent as well. He had come home with the purpose of being hired as a servant. However, his father had received him and reinstated him as a son. This confronted him with the challenge of overcoming his mind-set of guilt and unworthiness in order to embrace the person whom the father had declared him to be. Would he be able to receive the truth that could set him free? That was the dilemma he faced. He needed to repent, to allow his mind to be changed by the powerful truth that confronted him.

That is the dilemma we also face. On the one hand there is the persistent memory of the past with its failures, hurts, shame, and guilt. On the other hand there is the revelation of the gospel that shows me who I now am in Christ. In so many of our lives, the voice of condemnation drowns out the voice of revelation. It is so much easier to focus our eyes on us than on the Lamb. We become overwhelmed with the memory of our past rather than fixing our gaze on the robe, the ring, the sandals, the fatted calf—all symbols of our Father's grace lavished upon us. We walk down that dark road to find a corner in the servants' quarters.

Your journey to the Father's house begins with that first step of changing your mind about who you perceive yourself to be and who you truly are. When you do change your mind about who you are, you will change you mind about where you live, moving out of the cold and isolated quarters of the servant into the warmth and intimacy of the Father's house.

Father,

I repent of my wrong understanding of who you are
      and who you have declared me to be.
I repent of the lies I have believed that have kept me
    living in the servants' quarters,
      trying to earn your favor to receive a reward.
I ask your forgiveness for not having understood
    the mercy that you showed me
      when you saved me and called me your child.
I have allowed the enemy to convince me that I am unworthy
      to live in your house and sit at your table as a son or daughter.
I stand against the spirit of bondage, slavery, and servitude
      that has kept me in a performance trap of trying to please you.
And I ask the Holy Spirit, who is the Spirit of Adoption,
    to fill me with the joyful assurance of being
      a son and not a servant
And when I start to look at myself
    To lift my eyes to *Behold the Lamb!*

Conclusion

Now it happened as they went that He entered a certain village; and a certain woman named Martha welcomed Him into her house. And she had a sister called Mary, who also sat at Jesus' feet and heard His word. But Martha was distracted with much serving, and she approached Him and said, "Lord, do You not care that my sister has left me to serve alone? Therefore tell her to help me." And Jesus answered and said to her, "Martha, Martha, you are worried and troubled about many things. But one thing is needed, and Mary has chosen *that good part, which will not be taken away from her."*

Luke 10:38–42 (emphasis mine)

On my desk is an acorn-shaped covered dish. In that dish are some objects as significant in my life as the twelve stones at Gilgal and the single rock called Ebenezer. Call me sentimental, but I love to collect mementos from the places Bev and I have visited during forty-two years of ministry. In my bowl are nine shells and five stones. The seashells come from the beach at the mouth of the Igoda River where I encountered the grace of God in 1982. They are a constant source of gratitude as I think of how God met me and brought me out of the servants' quarters to take my rightful place in the Father's house.

The five stones come from a dusty spot on a lonely farm road in the middle of nowhere in Zimbabwe. What happened on that dusty spot was the watershed for my Jabbok encounter at Igoda River and for all the revelation of the truth in this book that set me free from the shackles of religious servitude into the freedom of living as a son. Why was that spot so important that ten years later, almost to the day, I drove back to that spot near Somabhula, Zimbabwe, and picked up those five stones that now rest on my desk?

It was there I looked up to heaven and prayed a decisive prayer that was the catalyst for changing my life. It came at the end of a struggle that followed my meditation on the story of Martha and Mary, where I discovered that I, like Martha, was wasting my life on the distractions of task-oriented ministry activities I thought were so important.

I could so identify with Jesus' assessment of distracted Martha. "Worried and troubled." That was me! The burden of pastoral ministry, meeting the expectations of the leadership and the church that I served, avoiding having Bev remind me of all the things I had not done—these things had left me worried and troubled and longing for some sort of escape. I felt like the missionary who told me, "If I could leave this mission field without losing face, I would be on a plane back to the States in a flash." Pride and the fear of what people would think kept me from just quitting and escaping.

"One thing is needed," Jesus said. Oh, for that simplification of my life. As I studied the last verse of Luke 10, an excitement began to build in me. Could it be that simple? Would making a choice as simple as Mary's rid me of the burden of years of misery, guilt, and fear?

"Mary has chosen that good part, which will not be taken away from her."

I wrote in my journal:

Like Martha, I feel that if I do the "one thing," how will the work get done? "Somebody has to be practical and keep their feet on the ground!" NO, JESUS DOES NOT WANT ME TO KEEP MY FEET ON THE GROUND BUT TO PUT MY FEET UP IN HIS PRESENCE!

As I continued to meditate, I felt the Holy Spirit offer me the same guarantee that Jesus had given to Mary: if I would choose for the rest of my life to sit at Jesus' feet and listen to his word, that place of rest and peace would never be taken from me.

What would that look like in my life? What would that entail? What would be the implications of making such a choice? These questions raced through my mind as I wound up my time of study in the Word and set out for a long walk on that ranch where I had spent so many happy hours with my family and friends. I set off walking south from the house down a long hill, over a creek, across a cattle grid and up the next hill. An excitement was building as I mulled over the decision that I felt the Lord was laying before me: did I really want to continue living like Martha, anxious and agitated, feeling all alone and abandoned by others who should have been helping me?

Emphatically no.

However, there is a security in the known, even if it is unbearable. The choice confronting me seemed fraught with risk. It was like signing a blank page and allowing God to fill in the details later.

Although the struggle was intense, the outcome was beyond doubt.

Fourteen years before, as a twenty-one-year-old sailing across the Atlantic Ocean from Rio de Janeiro to Cape Town, the quest of my life had crystallized. We were returning to South Africa from three months of ministry in South America. As part of a Youth for Christ "Teen-Team," we had sung and preached the gospel in Argentina, Chile, and Bolivia. During those twelve days at sea, Paul's longing in Philippians 3:10 became my longing: "[My determined purpose is] that I may know Him" (AMP).

In an ironic twist, two days out from Rio de Janeiro, the Arab-Israeli Six-Day War broke out. In less than a week it was over and the conflict ceased. In the same way, the conflict in me also ceased. The war for my heart had been won. Through all I had gone through, I sensed that God had been answering the cry of my heart. He had brought me to the end of my striving to be the best pastor, the best preacher, and the best church administrator with the best bedside manners. That was over.

Turning back down that long hill, I crossed over the cattle grid and came to a spot in the road just before the creek. I stopped and looked up to heaven and said, "Father, for the rest of my life, I choose, like Mary, to sit at Jesus' feet and listen to his word. I have no idea what the implications of this decision might be. I just know that I do not want to continue living as I have been. Today, by faith, I receive the same guarantee that you gave to Mary—that you will see to it that for the rest of my life I will be able to sit at his feet and listen to his word. I give you the freedom that whenever I get too busy or too distracted, you can stop me, call me aside, and restore me to that place of intimacy and rest."

That was my choice, the turning point, the beginning of the journey back to the Father's house.

So many of life's major turns start with simple choices. The young son in the parable made a choice: "Father, give me . . ." And with those words he started his long downhill journey to the far country.

After squandering his inheritance and nearly starving to death, he made a choice: "I will arise . . ." And with those words he began his journey home.

Choices.

Sinners choosing to come to Jesus and enjoy his company.

Pharisees choosing to stand aloof and criticize him.

The younger brother in the parable choosing to come home.

The older brother choosing to stay outside.

Martha choosing activity for Jesus over intimacy with him.

Mary choosing intimacy over activity.

Choices.

Each choice brought those people closer to God or took them farther away.

Which brings us to one final choice—*yours.*

Come out of the kitchen of religious activity, won't you? And sit at Jesus' feet. Mary's way of serving was so much more efficient than Martha's. If you sit still and listen well, Jesus will tell you what he wants, how much he wants, and when he wants it. That way, your activity for him will grow out of your intimacy with him instead of crowding out your intimacy with him.

Leave whatever far country you have been living in, won't you? And come home to the Father's house, where you will be welcomed, restored, and celebrated.

Leave whatever dutiful field you have been slaving in, won't you? And come join in the joy of your Father's heart, where there will be music and feasting and dancing!

A Closing Prayer from the Author

Dear Father,

Thank you for this time—this very sacred time—with the person
  who has read this book.
What a privilege it has been for me to share my journey
     from the servants' quarters to your house,
        from a life of activity to a life of intimacy,
           from the drudgery of simply doing to the joy of
           simply being your child.
Thank you for being so patient with me, Lord,
  as I made my way home.
Thank you for all the signposts along the way,
     for the Bible verses, the books, the speakers,
        all the pricks of conscience and the tugs of guidance.
I pray that the Holy Spirit would help the reader of this book
  to find his or her way home,
    whatever country he may be in,
      however far away it is,
        whatever he has wasted there;
whatever field she may be standing in,
    however aloof she is from you,
      however angry she is at you.

Embrace the man who has read this book.

Embrace the woman.

Shower them with kisses.

Bring them under the shelter of your roof,

>   where they may see how much you love them,

>   how much you cherish them,

>   how much you delight in them.

May all that has been lost . . . be found.

May all that has been squandered . . . be restored.

May all that has died . . . be brought back to life.

Even the joy.

Especially the joy.

>   In Jesus' name I pray,

>   amen

ACKNOWLEDGMENTS

Having a book published for the first time affords me a wonderful opportunity to share with readers the pictures of heroes and helpers who adorn the gallery of gratitude in my heart:

My father, Leslie Sheasby, through all the confusion of his theology and perfectionism, gave me an example of passionately pursuing Jesus, integrity, genuinely loving people, and showing loyalty to his friends. He passed on to me the family pioneering spirit, a love for the soil, the sea, and fast cars.

My mother, Daisy Sheasby, saintly, kind, gifted, faithful, and always serving. Her deathbed fear—"Have I done enough?"—spurred me on to preach the good news of *sola fide*.

Dad and Mom Wegener, Beverley's parents, who received me so warmly into the family and supported us in our moves—

first to war-torn Zimbabwe and then to faraway America. Their anonymous gifts paid for my theological education. Their generosity often rescued our family from hardship as they saw to it that we did not lack in the early years of ministry.

My family: Beverley, my amazing wife, to borrow a phrase from Melvin Udall in *As Good as it Gets*: "You make me want to be a better man." I would never be what I am today were it not for you. I am so thankful to God for giving me such a perfect gift. Tracy and Bradley, our two children, you are such a delight to a father's heart. You amaze me with the multitudinous gifts and abilities that have caused you to excel at every level. There is no limit for both of you in what you can accomplish and have fun doing. I am so grateful to God for healing you from the effects of my legalism and anger. I am so thrilled that the anger, perfectionism, performance, poverty, and religiosity that has been in our family for generations has stopped with me.

The visiting preachers for whom, through my childhood, I gave up my bed and who added to my life: Roger Voke, Jimmy Ferguson, Gypsy Williams, Clarrie Roux, and the amazing Reverend William Duma. Heinz Dedekind, who first opened my eyes to the doctrines of grace, and who taught me excellence in business, accuracy with accounting, and how to use levels and plumb lines to build a straight wall and an honest reputation in honor of the King. Dr. Jack Wiid, principal at Baptist Theological College of South Africa, who engendered in me a passion for the Greek language and accurate translation. Dr. Rex Mathie, who held me spellbound with his amazing gift of expository preaching and imparted to me a love of correct exegesis married to passionate declaration of truth. Ed Roebert, fellow pilgrim, pastor, and prayer partner, who challenged me to ask God for promises for my life and then boldly believe him for the fulfillment. Dr. Brian Russell, who was the singular encouraging voice among our peers when we felt God calling us to the United States. He spurred us on to launch out into the deep and trust God. Thank you, Brian.

Manley Beasley, man of faith, who risked so much in inviting an unknown preacher from Africa to come to the States. Dudley and T. D. Hall, who took me under their ministerial wings and facilitated the growth of Liberated Living Ministries as our first board members. Dudley, our conversations on grace and your skills in preaching the simplicity of grace, cemented the process of conversion from works-righteousness to "by grace through faith."

Bill James, for whom I drove trucks for nearly four years as God taught me to be a son. Thank you for providing me with the means to enjoy hours of conversation with my Father, who loved to be with me in the cabs of those trucks as I raced to make another delivery. Thank you for the many thousand-dollar donations added to my paycheck that sustained our family through those quiet years. You have been a faithful friend and a hero.

These heroes have a supporting cast of equally significant helpers: Mack and Dottie Kearney, Dr. Jimmy and Carol Ann Draper, David and Judy Neely, Jim and Gena Hough, Bob and Linda Murphy, Tom and Jean-Marie Sandy, Kenneth and Sharon Bond, Doug and Lari White, Jerry and Donna Smith, Winston and Julie Tan, Leah Springer, and "my three sons" Todd Bloom, Benjamin Dagley, and Jeff Whitley—they keep me young!

Last, I am so grateful to God for those involved with this project who have made this book a reality: Michael Blanton, you are an extraordinary man, and I am so blessed to have you as a friend and agent. You and Paula have enriched our lives through your friendship. Michael W. and Debbie Smith, thank you for your friendship and providing a platform for me to share the liberating message of sonship. Byron Williamson of Worthy Creative, thank you for believing that the message of sonship was worth the investment to bring this book to fruition. Rob Birkhead, thank you for your encouraging enthusiasm for this book. Ken Gire, you are a gift from the Father. Your empathy married to your skills as a wordsmith have enabled me to express myself way beyond my ability. You are the midwife who has helped me to give birth to this book so that many may discover the joy of living in the Father's house as sons and daughters.

NOTES

Chapter 7

1. Edith Schaeffer, "What Is a Father?" in *A Way of Seeing* (Grand Rapids, MI: Revell, 1977), 25.
2. Schaeffer, 25–26.
3. Schaeffer, 27.

Chapter 8

1. Personal correspondence to the author, January 19, 2008. Reprinted by permission.

Chapter 9

1. John Newton, "Come, My Soul, Thy Suit Prepare," in *Olney Hymns* (London: W. Oliver, 1779).

Share Your Thoughts

With the Author: Your comments will be forwarded to the author when you send them to *zauthor@zondervan.com*.

With Zondervan: Submit your review of this book by writing to *zreview@zondervan.com*.

Free Online Resources at
www.zondervan.com

Zondervan AuthorTracker: Be notified whenever your favorite authors publish new books, go on tour, or post an update about what's happening in their lives at www.zondervan.com/authortracker.

Daily Bible Verses and Devotions: Enrich your life with daily Bible verses or devotions that help you start every morning focused on God. Visit www.zondervan.com/newsletters.

Free Email Publications: Sign up for newsletters on Christian living, academic resources, church ministry, fiction, children's resources, and more. Visit www.zondervan.com/newsletters.

Zondervan Bible Search: Find and compare Bible passages in a variety of translations at www.zondervanbiblesearch.com.

Other Benefits: Register yourself to receive online benefits like coupons and special offers, or to participate in research.

ZONDERVAN®

ZONDERVAN.com/
AUTHORTRACKER
follow your favorite authors